Designed by Robert Budwig
Artwork by Pep Reiff, Typesetting by TypeArt
Origination by Peak Litho Plates Ltd., Tunbridge Wells
Printed in Italy by G. Canale & Co. SpA, Turin

ISBN 0-907305-68-7

The TOP ONE HUNDRED PASTA SAUCES

AUTHENTIC REGIONAL RECIPES from ITALY

BY DIANE SEED

ILLUSTRATED BY ROBERT BUDWIG

D

Dealerfield

Contents

For Antonio, who first taught me
to appreciate good pasta

Introduction

*P*asta has always been the glory of Italian food, and a symbol of Italian national pride. Today, Italian pasta, like Italian fashion, delights the world.

Nutritionists daily publish new support for 'the Mediterranean diet' as the healthiest and most natural food for us all, low in fat, moderate in protein, high in vitamins and carbohydrates. And that diet is founded on vegetables, fish, and pasta. Pasta itself is not fattening, though some sauces inspire caution. Cooks of many nationalities, whether offering unusual dishes for demanding friends, attempting to fill hungry families, or needing something fast after the office, frequently find they can solve their menu problems by turning to pasta. Pasta is infinitely varied: delicious, usually economical, largely vegetarian, can be fast and simple or complicated and extravagant according to mood.

Perhaps the one strength of which the non-Italian pasta cook is unaware is this variety. Even quite expert cooks often know only half a dozen pasta sauces. Yet the different regions of Italy yield many local specialities and numerous variations on national themes that have been tried and tested over generations. The fresh green vegetable sauces of Puglia in the southern 'heel' of Italy, the rich pork and tomato ragù of Naples, the delicate saffron and courgette-flower confection of the Abruzzi region, the aubergine recipes of Sicily, and the lemon sauces of the Amalfi coast all contribute to the amazing versatility of pasta as the foundation of innumerable meals. In the areas around Milan and Venice, traditionally dominated by rice, new pasta sauces are making increasing inroads. Italians eat pasta every day and they are not a people amused by monotony. Pasta has to appear in many guises to continue to arouse applause.

In this book, I have drawn together one hundred of the best pasta sauce recipes, encountered after many years of living, eating and cooking in Italy. Many of them are simple sauces that can be cooked in a few minutes. Others are elaborate confections from the kitchens of great Italian families. All of them adapt well to the needs of other countries, and other climates. However, it would be as well to remember that in Italy pasta is served as an entrée dish before the meat course, while outside Italy it is frequently thought of as the main course itself, and served with simply a salad to follow. In allowing for this, I have recommended quantities for all the pasta variations to feed four to six: an ample dinner for four hungry people, or sufficient for six elegant diners who will then move on to a meat course, as in Italy.

Diane Seed

How to serve pasta in the Italian style

Although pasta dishes are now eaten with equal enthusiasm from California to Australia, they often do not taste as good as they could outside Italy. But with time, and the knowledge of the following basic rules, we can all learn to perfect our pasta.

Top quality pasta

First and foremost, Italians make sure that the pasta itself takes priority and they know that no sauce, no matter how exquisite, will make the dish come right if the pasta itself is second-rate. This means buying good pasta to start with, from a reliable manufacturer of dried pasta or a high quality specialist shop making its own fresh pasta. If in doubt, I would always choose good quality dried pasta rather than doubtful or even stale 'fresh' pasta.

A pan for pasta

A very large, tall, good quality pan in which to boil sufficient water for the pasta is also a necessity: every 500 g (1 lb) of pasta needs to be cooked in at least 4 litres/7 pints/4 quarts of water and about 30 ml/2 tablespoons of salt. Bring the water to the boil and add the salt. With the water boiling briskly add the pasta all at the same time. Long pasta should be eased in and never broken. Stir the pasta every so often with a wooden fork to ensure that it stays separate. If I am using thick short pasta I usually add a few drops of olive oil to the boiling water before adding the pasta to prevent sticking. Bring the pasta and water back to the boil and boil briskly in an uncovered pan.

4

Timing: *the essential skill*

Italians fuss over perfectly cooked pasta as the French over a soufflé or the English over well-made tea. Pasta should always be firm and provide some resistance or 'bite', as the Italians say *'al dente'*. The old Neopolitan description was *'vierdi'* or 'green' as in slightly unripened fruit. Pasta, after all, is largely a texture.

In Italy no one dreams of adding the pasta to the boiling water until those who are going to eat it are actually present. Restaurants cook pasta freshly for every customer and do not understand impatient tourists who fret about the delay at the start of the meal. Instant pasta invariably means bad pasta so everyone should be prepared to wait for it to be freshly cooked. Pasta baked in the oven is the only kind that can be prepared in advance, which makes a dish like Baked pasta and Artichokes (p.31) ideal for formal entertaining.

Italian husbands about to leave their office telephone home to say, *"Butta la pasta"* – "throw in the pasta" – in other words, "I'm on my way". But woe betide the wife who takes him literally and actuallys starts to cook it before he is safely home. Overcooked pasta is rejected with a curl of the lip and the verdict, *"Scotta"* – overcooked – is a death sentence – to the pasta! Once overcooked it is always thrown away or given to the animals.

Most packets of dried pasta give directions for cooking, usually suggesting 8 to 10 minutes in boiling water. Egg pasta usually takes less time than flour and water pasta. For fresh pasta, ask the specialist shop what they recommend; 3 minutes or so is usually enough. But no Italian ever trusts such directions completely. An Italian never leaves the kitchen while the pasta is cooking and I have scandalised my Roman friends by occasionally walking away from the boiling pot for a second or two.

Unless you are an experienced cook it is best to make the sauce first and leave it on one side to be warmed only, or have a little cream stirred in while the pasta is cooking. You can then give the pasta the benefit of your full attention. Stand over the saucepan, and every so often lift out a strand or piece of pasta to nibble. When it is a little too hard, that is the moment to turn out the heat and drain the pasta. The time that this takes will finish the cooking. Some people recommend adding a few drops of cold water to stop the cooking process before draining, but if you have the colander and a heated serving bowl ready it should not be necessary. If you fear that you have left the pasta a fraction too long, add a few drops of cold water immediately and then drain.

Getting the proportion right

The proportion of sauce to pasta is also a crucial question involving some skill. Italians would criticise foreign cooks intent on producing the authentic dish for a superabundance of sauce. This is one area where 'the more the better' does not apply. The sauce is literally a sauce, intended to coat the pasta strands or shapes and add its flavour to every mouthful. But it should never become a soup, swilling around on the dish after the pasta has been eaten. In the following recipes, I have advised proportions that non–Italians may at first find stingy, and some cooks may prefer to increase the sauce quantities. But if the pasta is really well stirred (and for this a large bowl is very important) so that the pasta is very thoroughly coated with the accompanying sauce, this should not really be necessary.

Of course, the sauce is always competed for. And the last portion in the serving bowl is usually the most delicious. In a typical Roman *trattoria* the woman is served first and then the man is traditionally presented with his portion to eat directly from the serving bowl. When I finally rebelled and demanded my turn to eat from the serving bowl, the waiters received my request with consternation as if the last bastion of male privilege had been threatened.

Cheese: *the vital extra*

Few cooks outside Italy are aware either of the importance for the final flavour of mixing freshly cooked pasta with freshly grated Parmesan cheese *before* the addition of the sauce. This is not a process that is called for in every recipe, but it makes, for instance, Spaghetti Maria Grazia (page 42) a dish of pasta and courgette a memorable treat, while the combination without cheese or with cheese added at table might be much less interesting.

Needless to say, any cheese used with pasta must be freshly grated. Never use packets of ready-grated cheese. Parmesan cheese is expensive, but it is often the only extravagant item in the whole dish. Fresh Parmesan can be bought at most supermarkets and it will keep well wrapped in foil in the refrigerator. The best Parmesan will be marked 'Parmigiano-Reggiano' on the rind. Freshly ground black pepper is also a must in pasta dishes.

Pasta: *different ingredients and different shapes*

There are two kinds of pasta: that made with durum hard wheat flour and water, and that made with durum or soft flour and eggs. Both kinds of pasta can be dried and are sold in packets. Only soft flour and egg pasta is sold fresh or made at home, with one or two regional exceptions.

Hard Wheat and Water Pasta: Hard wheat and water pasta is used for round pasta strings such as spaghetti and is suited to olive oil based, robust sauces that make the pasta slippery and flavour it strongly with garlic and tomato. Since the durum wheat for this kind of pasta was grown around Naples, as early as the sixteenth century, Naples became the centre for the techniques of machine kneading and drying for wholesale consumption. Pasta dough made from durum wheat is too hard and brittle to knead by hand. Drying the hard pasta, always a tricky process since pasta dried too slowly goes mouldy and pasta dried too fast cracks and breaks, originally took place out of doors. The ancient streets and courtyards of old Naples were habitually strung not with washing but with pasta hung out to dry. The area around Torre Annunziata and Torre del Greco, where a combination of hot winds from Vesuvius and cool breezes from the sea were said to change the temperature four times a day, became the centre of the drying and later manufacture of pasta. Even today, gourmets seek out the small Dota factory near Naples where pasta dough is still shaped with rough edges, making it porous and more absorbent to the sauce. Filippo Porcelli, of Rome's 'Checco er Carretierre' restaurant, is one of a number of pasta connoisseurs who treks to Naples regularly to replenish his stocks of spaghetti from Dota.

In the Naples area, the appetite for macaroni as pasta was called, proved enormous from the start. Street vendors fished macaroni from boiling cauldrons, and sold it sprinkled with a little cheese and black pepper for a

mere two grani. This pasta was eaten with the fingers, the local populace throwing their heads back and raising their eyes to heaven as they lowered the strands into their mouths. Ingenuous foreign visitors marvelled at the sight and assumed that the poor were thanking God for their daily pasta.

Even aristocratic Neapolitans ate spaghetti with their hands and for this reason it was not served at court. Finally, Ferdinand II baulked at this deprivation, and his advisers invented the short four-pronged fork to allow their sovereign to eat his pasta with dignity. French chefs imported by the richest families – the Neapolitan name for 'chef' was *monzù*, a corruption of *monsieur* – had to learn to embellish pasta, and some of the meat sauces I have included as well as the 'special occasion' dishes show their influence.

Flour and Egg Pasta: Flour and egg pasta was invented in the rich pastures of the central Emilia-Romagna region of Italy. According to tradition, egg pasta made its first appearance in 1487 for the marriage of Lucrezia Borgia to the Duke of Ferrara, when the cook Zafirano wished to compliment her golden curls and rolled the pasta sheets into coils, cutting them into ringlets.

These delicate golden sheets of pasta, with 2 eggs to every 200 g/7 oz of flour, are used for most stuffed pasta, and cut into ribbons for tagliatelle and the thinner taglionini or tagliarini. Egg pasta is ideally suited to mild cream and butter-based sauces, with additions such as green asparagus, or ham and peas.

Ideas for Left Over Pasta

In Italy even the animals love pasta. Pet food manufacturers produce pasta for dogs, and in Rome every day one sees colonies of stray cats being fed left-over pasta.

Some leftovers are too tasty to be thrown away and they can be used to make delicious snacks or appetisers. I often make extra quantity spaghetti with pesto sauce so that I can use it the next day with beaten eggs to make a delicious omelette. Most pasta with a strongly flavoured sauce can also be fried directly in olive oil without eggs to make a crisp, brown round like a thick pancake.

But writing and reading about pasta and its tradition is hungry work. Let's make for the kitchen. *Butta la pasta!*

Please Note
All Recipes are for
4 people as a main course
or for 6 people
as a starter.

Basil
Basilico

*B*asil is the most important herb in Italian cooking. Its perfume enhances many dishes, and one of the best ways of serving pasta stuffed with spinach and ricotta is with a simple dressing of melted butter, Parmesan cheese and a few basil leaves. A salad of tomato and mozzarella cheese becomes food for the gods rather than slimmers when three or four basil leaves are tucked between the slices of tomato and mozzarella. In general, anything tomato benefits from the addition of a few leaves of basil.

Dried basil is not really an acceptable substitute, but before winter frosts kill off the plants it is possible to freeze some leaves to be used later in sauce-making. The flavour is best maintained by packing four or five leaves in a small plastic pot, such as an empty yogurt container. The leaves can then be covered with water and frozen. The frozen block can later be thawed out or added whole to a tomato sauce.

In Genoa, the birthplace of basil, and all along the Ligurian coast, the air is redolent of basil as every available space is filled with every available container, from old saucepans to beautifully painted ceramic pots. The Genovese believe that basil needs a gentle breeze from the sea to bring out its true flavour. Genoa was an independent maritime state, and the sea and the great seafarers like Christopher Colombus have influenced its culinary traditions. The most famous Genovese sauce, pesto, is made of basil which has been worked to form a durable, portable sauce, perfectly suited to long, hazardous voyages of discovery. It has been suggested that during the crusades, the Genovese contingent could be easily identified even as far afield as Jerusalem, by the characteristic aroma of pesto that surrounded them.

Although pesto can be bought ready-made its glory is appreciated when made at home. Originally, it was a slow, laborious procedure since the basil, garlic and nuts had to be pounded by hand in a pestle and mortar – hence the name 'pesto'. Now food processors and blenders have made it a simple task. Home-made pesto can be frozen very successfully during the summer months.

Pesto requires quite a large quantity of basil and this can provide difficulties in colder countries, but it is possible to grow your own, especially in a greenhouse or conservatory. Alternatively small packets can be bought in large supermarkets or ordered from specialists.

Trenette al Pesto
Trenette with Basil Sauce

500 g/1 lb trenette linguine or spaghetti
36 basil leaves (a minimum of 6 per person)
3 cloves garlic
150 g/5 oz pine nuts or walnuts or blanched almonds
100 g/4 oz (1¼ cups) freshly grated mixed pecorino
  romano and Parmesan cheese
200 ml/7 fl oz good quality olive oil
Salt and black pepper
3 small potatoes (optional)
175 g/6 oz green beans (optional)

Wipe the basil leaves with a damp cloth. Place the clean, dry leaves in the food processor together with the cloves of garlic. Turn on the machine and gradually add the nuts, then cheese and olive oil. Add salt and freshly ground black pepper.
Cook the pasta following packet directions carefully to avoid over-cooking.
It is usual to garnish the finished dish with slices of boiled potatoes and green beans around the edge of the serving plate. The potatoes are usually cooked with the pasta but it might be easier to boil two or three potatoes and the beans separately to get the timing right. This garnish is not essential but the potato does seem to make the flavour of the dish smoother.
The pesto sauce is never cooked but 2 or 3 tablespoons of pasta water should be added before the sauce is stirred thoroughly into the drained pasta. Make sure that every strand of pasta is coated with the sauce.
If you are using a large serving plate, arrange the slices of potatoes and the few green beans around the edge, with the pasta in the centre, and with a wooden spoon spread a little pesto over the vegetables. Serve at once.
Should there be any left-overs, a little spaghetti with pesto makes a delicious filling for the next day's omelette.

Walnuts
Noci

*W*alnuts go very well with pasta and cheese, and in Liguria it is customary to serve a walnut sauce with the herb and vegetable-stuffed pasta *pansooti* or ravioli. The following recipe was given to me by Mario who practises Genovese culinary arts in Rome's 'Taverna Giulia'. The sauce is very rich so if you are making this for a first course serve about six spinach and ricotta ravioli per person.

Ravioli con Salsa di Noci
Ravioli with Walnut Sauce

36 ravioli or other pasta stuffed with spinach and
   ricotta (6 per person)
50 g/2 oz (generous ½ cup) freshly grated Parmesan cheese
200 g/7 oz (about 1½ cups) shelled walnuts
200 ml/7 fl oz good quality olive oil
50 g/2 oz (4 tbsp) butter
100 ml/3½ fl oz double (heavy) cream
salt

This speedy sauce can be made in advance or while the pasta is cooking, whichever you prefer. Grate the cheese and put on one side. Chop the nuts in the food processor, then add the olive oil and butter. Next add the grated cheese, cream and salt to taste.
Cook the pasta, drain and coat with the sauce. I prefer to serve directly on to individual plates to avoid squashing the rather delicate cooked pasta.

Tagliatelle con Salsa di Noci
Tagliatelle with walnuts and mascarpone

500 g/1 lb tagliatelle
50 g/2 oz (4 tbsp) butter
1 clove garlic
200 g/7 oz (about 1½ cups) shelled walnuts
200 g/7 oz mascarpone or cream cheese
60 g/2½ oz (¾ cup) freshly grated Parmesan cheese

Melt the butter and fry the minced garlic until it is golden brown. Chop the nuts finely and add to the garlic and butter, stir for 3 minutes then remove from the heat.
Cook the pasta, following packet directions carefully to avoid over-cooking.
Add the cream cheese to the nuts and heat gently. Drain the pasta, toss in the grated Parmesan and transfer to a heated serving dish. Stir in the sauce and serve at once.

Aubergines
Melanzane

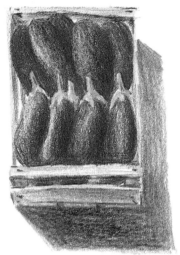

The Arabs first introduced aubergines (eggplants) – or *melanzane* to give them their Italian name – to Italy, and so it is in Sicily, where the Arab influence was strongest, that we find the treasure-house of aubergine recipes.

The traditional Sicilian aubergine pasta was re-christened 'Spaghetti alla Norma' in homage to the composer, Bellini, who was born in Catania. His great success with his opera, 'Norma', caused his proud fellow citizens to coin a new superlative, *'una vera Norma'* to describe and praise any form of excellence. This became so much a part of the local language that many years later the writer Nino Martoglio, tasting this succulent combination of aubergine and tomato for the first time, signalled his enthusiasm by calling it 'spaghetti alla Norma'. This new name, at first used only locally, has now become widespread throughout Italy.

Years ago while shopping in Rome's Testaccio market I was surprised to learn that the vegetable fennel has two sexes. The male fennel is round and fertile-looking while the so-called female fennel is longer and thinner. Having swallowed this, I learned recently that according to some experts aubergines, too, can be male or female, the male being the more desirable, the so-called male aubergine contains fewer seeds.

My neighbour, Angelina, who boasts of being fifth generation *contadina*, or agricultural worker, dismissed this theory rather scornfully as 'new-fangled nonsense', so I propose to follow her expert opinion and advise choosing aubergines for their freshness and not their sex. The aubergines should be shiny with a stretched look. Do not buy them if they are dull or wrinkled. The shape depends on the variety of aubergine, and round or long they taste the same.

Spaghetti con Melanzane e Noci
Spaghetti with Creamed Aubergines and Walnuts

500 g/1 lb spaghetti
3 large or 5 medium-size aubergines (eggplants)
3 eggs
15 walnut kernels
tomato sauce (half quantity of recipe page 36)
salt and black pepper
olive oil

Wash the aubergines, dry them and put them whole into a roasting tin. Cook in a hot oven for about 35 minutes until wrinkled and soft. Meanwhile, prepare the tomato sauce and hard boil the eggs until the yolks are just firm and creamy but not too floury. Shell the eggs and separate the yolks from the whites. Grind the walnuts. Halve the roasted aubergines and scrape the soft pulp into the ground walnuts. Mix well and add the egg yolks. Mix well again, then add the tomato sauce, salt and pepper to taste and a few drops of olive oil. Turn into a pan and heat for a few minutes, stirring all the time. Keep hot.
Cook the pasta, following the directions on the packet carefully so as not to overcook. Drain, turn into serving bowl and add the sauce.
Mix well and serve immediately.

Pasticcio di Maccheroni con le Melanzane
Baked Pasta with Aubergines

500 g/1 lb short pasta such as farfalle, tortiglioni, etc.
3 large or 5 medium aubergines (eggplants)
salt
tomato sauce (full quantity of recipe page 36)
flour
olive oil, approx 200 ml/7 fl oz
butter
300 g/10 oz mozzarella cheese

Cut and purge the aubergines as described in the third recipe. While they are 'purging' prepare the tomato sauce. Then flour and fry the slices as before. Cook the pasta in abundant boiling salted water, adding a few drops of oil to the water to avoid the pasta sticking together. Only cook the pasta for half the time stated in the packet directions or it will overcook in the oven. Drain the pasta, dress with a knob of butter and add the tomato sauce. Mix well.
Grease a deep ovenproof serving dish and spread a thin layer of pasta on the bottom. Cover this with a layer of fried aubergine slices, and cover these slices with thin slices of mozzarella. Repeat these layers until you have used up all your ingredients, finishing with a layer of mozzarella. Dot the top with butter and bake in a hot oven, 220°C/425°F/Mark 7 for 20 minutes until melted and golden brown.

Spaghetti alla Norma
Spaghetti Norma

500 g/1 lb spaghetti
5 medium-size or 3 large aubergines (eggplants)
salt
flour
olive oil for frying, approx 200 ml/7 fl oz
tomato sauce (full quantity of recipe page 36)
200 g/7 oz (2½ cups) freshly grated cheese, dry salted
    ricotta, Parmesan or pecorino romano

Top and tail the aubergines and slice them thinly. Arrange the slices in layers on a chopping board, sprinkling each layer with salt. Put the chopping board on the draining board, lifting one edge of the chopping board and wedging it so that it slopes slightly towards the sink. Then cover the slices of aubergine with a heavy weight (for example a large saucepan full of water) and leave for a couple of hours.
During this time a somewhat bitter liquid will drain from the aubergines.
In Italy this process is known as 'purging' the aubergines.
After 2 hours rinse the slices and pat dry. Lightly flour the slices to prevent them from absorbing too much oil when they are fried.
While the aubergines are 'purging' prepare the tomato sauce and grate the cheese. When the aubergines are drained and floured put a large saucepan of water on to boil for the pasta. While the water is heating, fry the aubergine slices in hot olive oil. Use plenty of oil and only fry a few slices at a time. Do not let them become too crisp. Drain each batch on kitchen paper and keep warm.
Warm the tomato sauce.
While you are frying the last few slices of aubergine, cook the pasta, following the directions on the packet very carefully to avoid overcooking. When it is ready, drain and put in a large serving bowl. Add first the cheese, mixing well, then the tomato sauce and finally the aubergines. Stir and serve immediately.

Lemons
Limone

*T*he first time I bought lemons with leaves it seemed to me a small miracle, and I get the same feeling every time I visit Amalfi, the famous lemon region, in the spring or summer months. The coastline is precipitous and the very narrow road has been carved out of the rock in an endless series of hairpin bends. There are tantalising glimpses of small churches with vivid mosaic domes, apricot and peach-coloured houses covered with bougainvillaea, and the blue, blue sea. In the few places where the road widens, local women have set up their stalls to sell bunches of Amalfi lemons to the passers-by. These lemons are large and thick-skinned, almost dimpled, and they are prized throughout Italy for their excellent flavour.

During the summer the 'Lemon Garden' restaurant in the town of Amalfi serves local lemon specialities at tables spread out under a natural canopy of lemon trees, the fruit hanging temptingly within reach. Small mozzarella cheeses are wrapped in aromatic lemon leaves and quickly barbecued. Here it is possible to eat one of the earliest spaghetti sauces. The spaghetti is boiled, drained and dressed with raw, finely-chopped garlic, parsley and freshly-squeezed lemon juice. This family recipe has been used for generations to counteract over-indulgence in rich food or as a remedy for other stomach upsets.

Over the years, this simple way of using lemon with pasta has been elaborated and more sophisticated lemon sauces have appeared in the cities.

Linguine al Limone
Linguine with Lemon Sauce

500 g/1 lb linguine or fine fresh pasta
2 lemons
250 ml/8 fl oz double cream (1 cup heavy cream)
100 ml/3½ fl oz grappa or acquavitae

Grate the coloured rind of one of the lemons and put on one side.
Remove the white pith and cut the fruit pulp into very small cubes. Squeeze juice
from the second lemon and keep separately. Put the cream, lemon cubes and grappa
into a pan and heat gently. Simmer until the sauce has become thicker.
Cook the pasta following the packet directions carefully to avoid over-cooking.
Remove the sauce from the heat and slowly add the lemon juice. Return to a low
heat to cook for 1 minute, stirring all the time.
Now add 2 teaspoons of grated lemon rind, stir well and pour over the drained
pasta. Mix the sauce into the pasta and turn into a heated serving bowl.
Put a few strands of lemon rind on top and serve.

Tagliolini al Limone
Tagliolini with Lemon Sauce

This sauce was created by Giuseppe Palladino for his lovely
Roman restaurant, 'Vecchia Roma'.

500 g/1 lb tagliolini (tagliarini), preferably fresh
1 clove garlic
25 g/1 oz (2 tbsp) butter
1.25 ml/¼ tsp crushed, dried chilli pepper flakes
2 lemons
100 g/4 oz cooked ham
500 ml/16 fl oz double cream (2 cups heavy cream)
salt

Mince or chop the garlic into minute pieces. Melt the butter and gently fry the garlic
until it is golden brown. Add the crushed chillies. Wash the lemons and grate the
coloured rind or zest very finely, being sure not to grate the tough white skin which
will make the sauce bitter. If you use a zester the fine threads of lemon can also serve
as a garnish.
Cut the ham into fine matchsticks, and add to the garlic and butter. Heat gently,
then add the lemon rind and the cream. Simmer uncovered for just under 1 hour.
Heat a large pan of water and when it comes to the boil throw in the tagliolini.
Drain it immediately because this process is not to cook the pasta, only to make it
more flexible and less fragile.
Turn the sauce into a large pan and add the drained pasta. Cook the pasta gently in
the sauce for the required time, usually very few minutes. Add salt to taste.
Add a little more cream if the sauce has become too dense, but be careful not to
'drown' the pasta. Turn into a heated serving dish, decorate the top with fine threads
of lemon rind and serve at once.

Garlic, Olive oil, Chilli

Aglio, olio e peperoncini

*M*y introduction to this famous pasta dish occurred when I overheard two elderly priests discussing the pros and cons of Spaghetti alla Puttanesca – *Whore's spaghetti* – as they deliberated over the menu in a Neapolitan restaurant. Made of ingredients found in most Italian larders, this is also known as 'Spaghetti alla Buona Donna' – or Good Woman's spaghetti – which can be misleading if one is not familiar with the ironic insult *'figlio d'una buona donna'* – son of a good woman.

To understand how this sauce came to get its name we have to look back to the 1950's when brothels in Italy were state-owned. They were known as *case chiuse* or 'closed houses' because the shutters had to be kept permanently closed to avoid offending the sensibilities of neighbours or innocent passers-by. Conscientious Italian housewives always shop at the local market every day to buy really fresh food, but the 'civil servants' were only allowed one day per week for shopping and their time was valuable. Their speciality became a sauce made quickly from odds and ends in the larder and now invaluable to us all, of whatever degree of virtue, when time and ingredients are in short supply.

Spaghetti alla Puttanesca

Whore's spaghetti

500 g/1 lb spaghetti or vermicelli
salt
20 ml/1½ tbsp olive oil
3 cloves garlic
3 anchovy fillets
400 g/14 oz tin Italian plum tomatoes
120 g/4 oz (1 cup) pitted black olives
60 ml/4 tbsp capers
parsley

Cook the pasta in a large saucepan of boiling salted water following the directions on the packet carefully to avoid overcooking. While the water for the pasta is heating put the olive oil in a frying pan. Add the finely chopped garlic and chopped anchovy fillets and cook gently until they are almost melted. Now stir in the chopped tomatoes with their juice, the black olives and capers. (These can be chopped or left whole according to taste but if the olives are large it is better to chop them.)
Cook for 5 minutes.
When the pasta is ready, drain it and add the sauce. Mix well, sprinkle with chopped parsley and serve immediately.

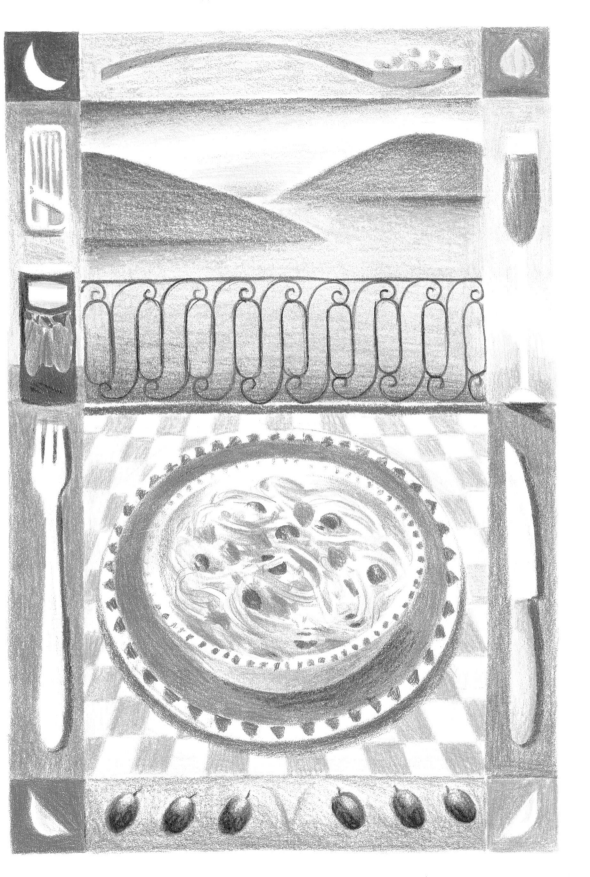

Spaghetti Aglio, Olio e Peperoncino
Spaghetti with Garlic, Olive Oil and Chilli Pepper

This very basic sauce is traditionally served in the late, late hours, often after a formal reception or the opera as an impromptu snack for anyone feeling suddenly peckish. Often it is the elegant host who removes his jacket to prepare this instant nourishment for his guests.

500 g/1 lb spaghetti
salt
100 ml/6 tbsp olive oil
5 cloves garlic
1 small chilli pepper
parsley (optional)

Cook the pasta in boiling salted water, following the directions on the packet carefully to avoid overcooking.
Meanwhile, heat the olive oil and add the garlic. This is either left whole and removed before serving or it is finely chopped and not removed. Add the chilli pepper which has been cut into 3 or 4 pieces, cook until the garlic is golden brown.
The moment the pasta is ready, drain it and put into a large serving bowl.
Remove the the chilli and garlic, if left whole, from the oil and pour the sizzling oil over the pasta, stirring well. There must be sufficient oil to coat every strand of pasta and make it slippery and shiny. Add chopped parsley if desired and serve immediately.
This simple sauce can even be prepared omitting the chilli pepper if a less spicy dish is desired. In this case freshly ground black pepper is added after the hot oil has been stirred into the pasta.
Another sauce can be prepared by altering the previous recipe as follows: replace the chilli with 2 50 g/2 oz tins of anchovy fillets, drained and chopped into small pieces; reduce the quantity of garlic to 2 cloves, left whole and removed once brown; add 60 ml/4 tbsp of the pasta water to the finished dish and stir well.

Spaghetti Indiavolati
Devilled Spaghetti

This variation on oil, garlic and chilli gets is name from the small, very hot chilli peppers called *diavolicchi* – 'little devils'. A rather unusual method of infusion is used. The garlic and chilli are not fried and the final dish is thus lighter and more digestible.

500 g/1 lb spaghetti
6 cloves garlic
2 small very hot red chilli peppers
salt
50 ml/3 tbsp olive oil
50 g/2 oz (generous ½ cup) freshly grated Parmesan cheese
parsley (optional)

Grind up the garlic and chillies in a blender with 500 ml/16 fl oz of water. Bring a large saucepan of salted water to the boil and add the mixture from the blender. Bring back to the boil and simmer gently for 15 minutes.
Pour the contents of the saucepan through a fine sieve into another pan and check to make sure that there is enough liquid to cook the pasta. If not, add more water. Discard the garlic and chillies.
Bring to the boil again and add the spaghetti. Cook following the directions on the packet carefully to avoid overcooking. Drain and dress with the olive oil and the freshly grated cheese. Chopped parsley may be added if a touch of colour is desired.

Spaghetti Siracusani

Spaghetti Syracuse

Named after the Sicilian town of Syracuse, this is again made from ingredients
usually found in every Italian kitchen.

500 g/1 lb spaghetti or vermicelli
1 large aubergine (eggplant)
salt
2 sweet peppers, yellow if available
400 g/14 oz can Italian plum tomatoes
4 anchovy fillets
30 ml/2 tbsp capers
12 pitted black olives
20 ml/2 tbsp olive oil
3 cloves garlic
a few basil leaves, if available
40 g/1½ oz (½ cup) freshly grated Parmesan cheese

Cut the aubergine into medium-thick slices and leave to 'purge' (see page 16).
Meanwhile, roast the peppers in a very hot oven, 230-240°C/450-475°F/Mark 8-9,
for 20 minutes; the skins should become quite discoloured. (Italian housewives char
the pepper skins over the naked flame on top of a gas stove, using a fork to hold the
pepper in position, but I always end up with burnt fingers, black peppers and a filthy
gas stove so I prefer the oven method.) Remove the peppers from the oven and place
them in a paper bag until they become cool. It should now be quite easy to remove
the skin which is rather indigestible. Remove the seeds from the peppers and cut
them into small strips.
Rinse the aubergine slices and pat dry. Cut the slices into small cubes.
Drain the tomatoes and chop them. Chop the anchovy fillets and the capers.
Chop the black olives if they are very large.
Heat the olive oil and add the finely chopped garlic, anchovies, aubergine and
tomatoes. Cook gently for about 10 minutes, then add the capers, olives, peppers
and basil. Cover and cook for about 15 minutes. Check for seasoning.
During this time cook the pasta, following the directions on the packet carefully to
avoid overcooking. Drain the pasta and put it into a large serving bowl.
Add the sauce and stir rapidly to coat all the pasta with the sauce.
Add the freshly grated cheese, stir and serve.

Mushrooms
Funghi

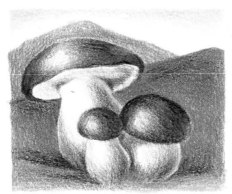

*I*n Italian cooking, mushrooms in one form or another appear everywhere on the menu except the sweet course. They make light, tasty appetisers, delectable pasta sauces, a sumptuous main course – the great roast *porcini* mushrooms served whole in all their splendour – a refreshing, crisp salad ingredient, and sliced or *trifolato* as a harmonising accompaniment to meat or fish dishes.

The most sought-after variety of mushroom is the funghi *porcini*, literally 'little pigs'. This is the cep or *Boletus edulis* which looks so repulsive but tastes so divine. In season they are displayed (uncooked) in local restaurants as a sort of Salvador Dali still life, and their high cost ensures that they are handled as reverently as a work of art. The waiters proudly exhibit them to the potential customer and the choice follows a painstaking inspection which is only equalled by the care with which an *inteditore* or knowledgeable client examines the gills and eyes of the fish on display before selecting what shall be cooked for him.

Out of season, dried *porcini* are used to make sauces and they prove a very acceptable substitute for fresh, especially in sauces with other ingredients. Packets of dried mushrooms are exported from Italy and may be used with confidence. Soak the dried mushrooms in tepid water for 15 minutes.

The pasta sauce, known as *carrettiere*, or carter's sauce, uses a very interesting combination of dried *porcini*, tomato and tuna fish and can be enjoyed at Rome's trastevere restaurant Checco er Carrettiere. Checco, the grandfather of the present owner, Filippo Porcelli, used to drive his cart to the Castelli area outside Rome to transport wine back to the thirsty city. Today the twenty odd kilometres seem nothing to any Roman wanting to escape for an evening from Rome's torrid summer heat, but by horse and cart it was an arduous journey, especially when laden down by great quantities of wine. Grandmother Margherita thought up the following recipe as a sustaining one-course meal for the men of her family.

Tagliatelle alla Boscaiola

Forester's style Tagliatelle

Any Italian dish with the name *boscaiola* includes mushrooms in some form.

> 500 g/1 lb tagliatelle or spaghetti
> 45 ml/3 tbsp olive oil
> 3 cloves garlic
> 400 g/14 oz tinned Italian plum tomatoes
> salt and black pepper
> 300 g/10 oz fresh mushrooms, or dried equivalent
> parsley

Heat two-thirds of the olive oil and add the finely chopped garlic. When it begins
to turn colour add the tomatoes with their juice, squashing them with a wooden
spoon. Add salt and pepper to taste. Cook briskly for 15 minutes.
Meanwhile, heat the rest of the oil in a separate pan and add the mushrooms which
have been wiped with a damp cloth and then finely sliced. Lightly salt the
mushrooms and let them cook gently for 5 minutes. Add the chopped parsley
and keep warm.
Cook the pasta, following packet directions carefully to avoid over-cooking.
Drain the pasta and turn into a heated serving dish. Add the tomato sauce,
stirring thoroughly, and then the mushrooms. Stir well and serve at once.

Bucatini con i Funghi

Bucatini with Mushrooms

This pasta dish can only be made with fresh mushrooms.

> 500 g/1 lb bucatini or spaghetti
> 15 ml/1 tbsp olive oil
> 2 cloves garlic
> 300 g/10 oz fresh mushrooms
> salt and black pepper
> 15 ml/1 tbsp lemon juice
> parsley

Heat the oil and add the finely chopped garlic. Now add the mushrooms which
have been wiped with a damp cloth and then finely sliced. Add a little seasoning,
then cover the pan and leave to cook for 5 minutes over a low heat, then remove
and keep warm. The mushrooms should give out enough moisture to cook
themselves gently.
Cook the pasta, following packet directions very carefully to avoid over-cooking.
Add the lemon juice and chopped parsley to the mushrooms and stir into the
drained pasta. Mix thoroughly, adding a little more olive oil if desired.
Serve at once.

Spaghetti alla Carrettiere

Carter's style Spaghetti

500 g/1 lb spaghetti or tagliatelle
250 g/8 oz mushrooms, fresh or dried
45 ml/3 tbsp olive oil
2 cloves garlic
1 small chilli pepper, or 5 ml/1 tsp crushed
    dried chilli pepper flakes
100 g/4 oz bacon
400 g/14 oz tinned Italian plum tomatoes
80 g/3 oz tinned tuna fish
Parsley

Wipe the fresh mushroom caps with a damp cloth and slice finely.
Soak dried mushrooms, drain and slice. Heat the oil and add the finely chopped
garlic and chilli pepper. When the garlic begins to change colour add the bacon
cut into small cubes. When the fat begins to melt from the bacon
add the mushrooms and, after 5 minutes, the drained tomatoes.
After 15 minutes on a low heat add the well-drained and flaked tuna fish.
Cook gently for another 15 minutes.
During this time, cook the pasta following packet directions carefully to avoid
over-cooking . Drain the pasta, turn into a heated serving dish and stir in the
mushroom sauce, mixing well.
Add the chopped parsley and serve at once.

Artichokes
Carciofi

The Arabs brought the globe artichoke to Italy, and its Italian name *carciofi* is a phoneticized version of the arabic *kharciof*. Artichokes enjoyed great popularity at the Medici court, and during the Renaissance the artichoke was believed to be an aphrodisiac. In modern Italy it is prized for its high iron and iodine content and its beneficial effect on the liver.

The artichoke appears in many different guises in modern Italian gastronomy. Minute whole pickled artichokes – *carciofini* – appear as antipasto or as snack-bar sandwich fillings. In Rome, young tender artichokes without a choke are cooked in oil, white wine and mint. Every

28

part of this artichoke can be eaten and it looks spectacular as it is presented standing on its head with its long stalk in the air. In the old ghetto area, near Marcello's theatre, the same young artichokes are cooked *all giudia* – 'in the Jewish way' – the whole artichoke pressed open until it resembles a water lily. Deep fried, every delicious, crunchy morsel can be eaten. Artichokes are even used to make an aperitivo – 'Cynar'. The manufacturers claim that this drink alleviates the stress of frantic modern life.

However, the real wealth of the artichoke is best seen in pasta recipes. Although it is difficult to find the small tender artichokes outside the climate of Italy or California, it is quite easy to obtain the purple-leaved spiky variety which can be used almost as well.

In my Rome market I buy fresh artichokes which have been trimmed and prepared by the vegetable seller, each artichoke rubbed with lemon to stop it going brown. Artichokes turn brown very quickly once they are cut so prepare an acid mixture of water and vinegar or lemon juice before beginning an artichoke-based pasta sauce. Artichokes can also stain the hands quite badly so I advise rubber gloves for the cleaning and chopping.

Preparing Artichokes

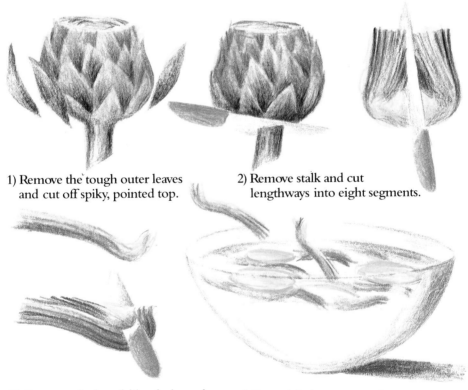

1) Remove the tough outer leaves and cut off spiky, pointed top.

2) Remove stalk and cut lengthways into eight segments.

3) Cut away the beard-like choke and discard any tough leaves that might spoil the sauce.

4) Put artichoke segments into water with vinegar or lemon to prevent discolouration.

Cannelloni ai Carciofi
Cannelloni with Artichoke

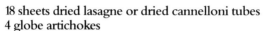

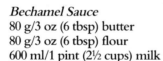

18 sheets dried lasagne or dried cannelloni tubes
4 globe artichokes
50 ml/3½ tbsp olive oil
1 onion
2 cloves garlic
250 g/8 oz minced (ground) veal
100 ml/3½ fl oz (½ cup) dry white wine
5 ml/1 tsp chopped thyme
salt and black pepper
200 ml/⅓ pint (1 cup) chicken stock
1 egg yolk
80 g/3 oz (1 cup) freshly grated Parmesan cheese

Bechamel Sauce
80 g/3 oz (6 tbsp) butter
80 g/3 oz (6 tbsp) flour
600 ml/1 pint (2½ cups) milk

Prepare the artichokes and put them in a bowl of lemon water, as explained in the introductory paragraph. Just before using them, drain and chop.

Heat the oil and gently fry the finely chopped onion and garlic for 5 minutes. Add the artichokes and veal, stir well and leave to cook over a very gentle heat for 10 minutes. Pour in the white wine and cook for another 10 minutes. Season with the thyme, salt and freshly ground pepper. Cover and simmer for 15 minutes, adding a little of the stock from time to time to keep the mixture moist.

Meanwhile, make a thick bechamel sauce with the butter, flour and milk. Season well. Mince (grind), or process the artichoke mixture at the end of the cooking time, then add the egg yolk, half the freshly grated cheese and about 100 ml/¼ pint (⅓ cup) of bechamel sauce. This mixture is used to stuff the cannelloni.

If using lasagne sheets, cook them as in the previous recipe. Prepare the cannelloni tubes carefully following the packet directions.

If using lasagne, place a little filling on one side of each sheet and then roll up to make a tube. Place the stuffed pasta in a buttered, rectangular oven dish, with the seam at the bottom. If you need to make a second layer, brush the first layer with butter before adding the second. Pour the rest of the bechamel sauce over the filled cannelloni and sprinkle with the rest of the cheese. Bake in a hot oven, 220°C/425°F/ Mark 7, for about 20 minutes.

Tagliatelle al Carciofi
Tagliatelle with Artichokes

500 g/1 lb tagliatelle
4 globe artichokes
30 ml/2 tbsp olive oil
30 g/1 oz (2 tbsp) butter
1 small onion
150 ml/¼ pint (⅔ cup) dry white wine
juice of ½ lemon
150 ml/¼ pint (⅔ cup) chicken or beef stock
200 ml/⅓ pint double cream (1 cup heavy cream)
salt and black pepper
40 g/1½ oz (½ cup) freshly grated
    Parmesan cheese

Prepare the artichokes and put in a bowl of vinegar water as explained in the introduction. Just before using them, drain and chop.
Heat the oil and butter and gently fry the chopped onion until soft. Keep the heat low and cover the pan. After about 5 minutes add the chopped artichokes. Stir, cover again and cook for another 5 minutes. Now add the white wine, lemon juice and stock. Cook gently, covered, for about 20 minutes.
Meanwhile, heat the water for the pasta. Once you have added the pasta to the water, stir the cream into the artichoke mixture and leave uncovered on a very low heat. Season with salt and freshly ground pepper. The sauce will become thick while the pasta is cooking. Be certain not to overcook the tagliatelle.
Drain the pasta and immediately stir in the freshly grated cheese so that all the pasta is coated with the cheese. Now pour on the artichoke sauce and stir vigorously.
Serve at once.

Spaghetti o Penne con i Carciofi
Spaghetti or Penne with Artichokes

500 g/1 lb spaghetti or penne
4 large globe artichokes
50 ml/3½ tbsp olive oil
2 cloves garlic
30 ml/2 tbsp chopped parsley
salt and black pepper
Parmesan cheese

Prepare the artichokes as explained in the introducion. Just before using, drain and chop. Heat the oil and add the chopped garlic.
Add the artichokes and cover thepan so that they stew rather than fry. When they are nearly cooked (usually about 20 minutes, but less if the artichokes are really young and tender), add the parsley and salt and pepper to taste. Keep warm.

Cook the pasta, following the packet directions carefully to avoid overcooking. Drain the pasta, reserving about 60 ml/4 tbsp of the pasta water. Turn the pasta into a large serving bowl and quickly stir in the artichokes and the reserved pasta water. Serve immediately. A bowl of freshly grated Parmesan cheese should be served separately for those who like to add cheese.

Pasticcio di Carciofi

Baked Pasta and Artichokes

9 sheets dried lasagne
6 globe artichokes
30 ml/2 tbsp olive oil
80 g/3 oz (6 tbsp) butter
1 onion
small glass of dry white wine
5 ml/1 tsp chopped thyme
100 g/4 oz (1¼ cups) freshly grated Parmesan
Bechamel Sauce
70 g/3 oz (6 tbsp) butter
70 g/3 oz (4½ tbsp) flour
700 ml/1¼ pints (3 cups) milk
salt, pepper, nutmeg

Prepare the artichokes and put in a bowl of lemon water, as explained in the introductory paragraph. Just before using, drain well.
Heat the oil and butter and add the finely chopped onion. Cover and cook for about 5 minutes. Place the artichoke segments in the pan and stir for about 5 minutes. Pour in the wine and season with salt to taste and the thyme. Cover and cook gently for about 20 minutes.
While the artichokes are cooking, heat a large saucepan of water. Salt well and cook the lasagne, one or two sheets at a time, in the boiling water for about 5 minutes. Remove with a slotted spoon and plunge instantly into a bowl of cold water. Remove from the cold water and lay out on a clean towel. Although this process is time-consuming it is necessary to prevent the sheets of pasta sticking together. Make a bechamel sauce with the butter, flour, milk and seasonings.
Butter a rectangular oven dish and pour in one quarter of the bechamel sauce. Cover this with three sheets of lasagne, overlapping them a little. Pour in one third of the remaining bechamel to cover the pasta, and sprinkle one third of the freshly grated cheese over this. Now add half the artichoke mixture, spreading it evenly over all the surface. Cover this with another three sheets of lasagne. Pour on half the remaining bechamel sauce and again sprinkle with cheese, using half the remainder. Spread the last of the artichoke mixture evenly over this. Cover with the three remaining sheets of lasagne and the rest of the sauce and cheese.
Dot with remaining butter.
Bake in a hot oven, 220°C/425°F/Mark 7, for about 30 minutes.
Remove from the oven and let the dish 'settle' for about 3 minutes before serving.

Tomato

Pomodoro

*H*ard though it is to imagine Italy without the tomato, that fruit was only brought to Europe in the sixteenth century from voyages of discovery to Mexico and Peru. Because its iron and vitamin content was seen to impart a lusty vigour, the tomato was first known as *pomme d'amour* or 'love apple'. The name eventually became changed to *pomme d'or* or 'golden apple', evoking memories of the Hesperides myth, and in Italy the name *pomodoro* is still used today.

During the summer one can find at least four types of tomatoes in local markets in Italy. The unripe orangey-green tomatoes are preferred for salad while the large, round red tomatoes are used mainly stuffed with rice. The tomato used for sauce is the San Marzano, the plum tomato that it is also tinned and exported all over the world. In the south, the small round cherry tomato is also used for a pasta sauce.

Even in the cities the Italian housewife buys fresh tomatoes daily throughout the summer to make her sauce. In September, large crates of tomatoes (popularly known as *oro rosso* or 'red gold') are sold by the roadside and every Fiat seems in danger of being crushed under the weight of the crates of tomatoes stacked on top. The great task of making enough bottled tomatoes to last the winter begins. Whole families – grandparents, fathers, mothers, children – gather together to help in the yearly ritual. The washed tomatoes are put through a simple apparatus that removes the skin and seeds. The resulting purée is poured into clean beer or mineral water bottles, and usually a leaf or two of basil is added before the bottles are capped and sterilized in a seething cauldron of boiling water. This procedure is nearly always carried out in the open air and driving through the countryside one comes upon small, brilliant red 'rivers' where the grass and earth have been stained with the huge quantity of skins and seeds thrown out by the primitive pulping machines.

This filtered purée is known as *passato* and even today, when it can be bought already bottled, a large proportion of the populace take pride and pleasure in this personal replenishment of the storecupboard.

In Puglia and Magna Grecia, the ancient method of drying tomatoes in the hot Southern sun is still used. These dried tomatoes can be bought in small glass jars in speciality shops. They have a very strong, concentrated flavour and are perhaps an acquired taste.

Tinned, peeled tomatoes known as *pelati* are also used to make pasta sauce and are the first resort of most cooks outside Italy. The hot sun gives a unique flavour to Italian tomatoes. Even the same variety grown in northern climates would not have the same taste and it would be a mistake to try to use them for pasta sauces. Always use tinned Italian tomatoes in preference to a fresh Northern variety. If you do happen to have fresh plum tomatoes, remove the skins by plunging them into boiling water for a few minutes. Allow slightly less cooking time because there will be less liquid to evaporate.

There are many different versions of tomato sauce and every Italian family has its own favourite. Some prefer to leave the garlic and onion whole, removing the garlic at the end of the frying time and the onion before sieving the final sauce. (The onion is then usually much in demand as a tasty titbit!) Some cooks add a small piece of celery, finely chopped, with the onion and garlic, others add celery and chopped carrot. I have known families who add a good spoonful of brandy to the nearly-finished sauce (rather like the Italian habit of adding brandy, or other liqueurs, to their morning black expresso coffee, which is then called *caffè coretto* or 'corrected coffee'!), while others content themselves with adding a generous dose of good red wine.

No two tomato sauces are ever identical. This is generally accepted, and in Sicily there is even an expression to describe a changeable personality: *Cambia sempre come la salsa* – 'He is always different, like a sauce'.

Tagliatelle o Spaghetti al Pomodoro
Tagliatelle or Spaghetti with Tomato Sauce

500 g/1 lb tagliatelle or spaghetti
30 ml/2 tbsp olive oil
1 medium onion
2 cloves garlic
2 400 g/14 oz cans Italian plum tomatoes
1 sugar lump
salt and black pepper
60 g/2 oz (1 cup) freshly grated Parmesan cheese

Heat the oil and gently fry the chopped onion and garlic until softened. I usually cover the pan to prevent browning. Add the tomatoes with their juice, sugar, salt and freshly ground pepper to taste and cook on a high flame, uncovered, for about 20 minutes, stirring occasionally. When the sauce is reduced and thick, check the seasoning, then pass the sauce through the medium disc of a food mill. (Although not authentic, you can also use an electric blender or food processor to save time.)
Cook the pasta, following the directions on the packet very carefully to avoid overcooking. Drain the pasta and add half the freshly grated cheese, stirring thoroughly. Then add the sauce. Stir well, add the rest of the cheese and serve.

Tagliatelle al Pomodoro e Basilico
Tagliatelle with Tomato and Basil

This sauce is only worth making if you have fresh basil. Basil leaves lose much of their perfume if they are washed in water; they should just be wiped gently with a slightly moist kitchen towel.

500 g/1 lb tagliatelle or spaghetti
30 ml/2 tbsp olive oil
2 400 g/14 oz cans Italian plum tomatoes
salt and black pepper
8 basil leaves
40–60 g/1½–2 oz (½–¾ cup) freshly grated
  Parmesan cheese (optional)

Heat the oil and add the tomatoes with their juice, squashing them in the pan with a fork. Cook rapidly for 5 or 10 minutes, not longer, to retain the fresh vivid red colour. Add salt and pepper to taste and the whole basil leaves. Stir well.
Cook the pasta in boiling salted water following the directions on the packet to avoid overcooking. Drain the pasta the moment it is ready, add the sauce, toss and serve.
This sauce is usually served without cheese, but if you like, add the freshly grated Parmesan to the pasta and stir thoroughly before you add the sauce.

Penne all Arrabbiata

Pasta Quills with Fiery Sauce

This sauce seems to have developed in the Forties and is believed to owe its origin to Italy's Libyan campaign and the soldiers' introduction to hot, peppery Arab cooking.

> 500 g/l lb penne or spaghetti
> Tomato sauce (full quantity of recipe page 36)
> 1 small chilli pepper or 5 ml/1 tsp dried crushed
>   chillies (hot red pepper flakes)
> 30 ml/2 tbsp chopped parsley

Make the tomato sauce, adding the chopped chilli pepper to the garlic and onions and frying gently before adding the tomatoes. Traditionally, quill-shaped pasta, such as penne is used, but the sauce goes well with any packet pasta. It is not good with fresh pasta. Add the freshly chopped parsley before serving. Cheese is not usually served with this sauce.
Some versions of this 'rabid' sauce include 125 g/4 oz bacon in the initial frying, but I prefer the tangy healthy Roman version with no animal fat.

Spaghetti al Pomodoro e Arancia

Spaghetti with Tomato and Orange Sauce

> 500 g/l lb spaghetti
> 15 ml/1 tbsp olive oil
> 1 clove garlic
> 3 sprigs parsley
> 4 basil leaves, if available
> 2 400 g/14 oz cans Italian plum tomatoes
> salt
> juice of 1 orange

Heat the oil and add the slightly crushed garlic and whole herbs. Stir and add the tomatoes with their juice, crushing them with a fork in the pan. Add salt to taste and cook rapidly for 10 to 15 minutes, stirring occasionally.
Add the orange juice to the sauce and cook for another 3 minutes. Remove the garlic and herbs and blend or process the sauce. Keep warm.
Cook the pasta in boiling salted water carefully following the directions on the packet to avoid overcooking. Drain the pasta, toss with the sauce and serve.
Cheese is not served with this recipe.

Spaghetti Vesuvio
Spaghetti with Vesuvius Sauce

500 g/1 lb spaghetti
15 ml/1 tbsp olive oil
2 400 g/14 oz cans Italian plum tomatoes
5 ml/1 tsp dried oregano
salt
50 g/2 oz (generous ½ cup) freshly grated
   Parmesan cheese
200 g/7 oz mozzarella cheese

Warm the oil and add the tomatoes with their juice, squashing them in the pan with a fork. Add the oregano and salt to taste and cook rapidly for 20 minutes. While the sauce is cooking, chop the mozzarella into small cubes. Cook the pasta, taking care to follow the directions on the packet to avoid overcooking. When the pasta is ready, drain and add the freshly grated Parmesan, the tomato sauce and the diced mozzarella. Toss rapidly, then cover and leave for about 3 minutes so that the mozzarella begins to melt and look like streams of molten lava. Serve hot.

Bucatini o Spaghetti alla Sorrentina
Bucatini with Sorrento Sauce

This recipe from Sorrento is similar to the previous one, again influenced by Vesuvius' volcanic eruptions.

500 g/1 lb bucatini or spaghetti
tomato sauce (full quantity of recipe page 36)
60 g/2½ oz (5 tbsp) butter
250 g/8 oz mozzarella cheese
50 g/2 oz (generous ½ cup) freshly grated
   Parmesan cheese

This is traditionally made with bucatini, but I prefer the finer, more slippery spaghetti.
Make the tomato sauce, but use the butter instead of olive oil. While the sauce is cooking, cook the pasta, carefully following the directions on the packet to avoid overcooking.
When the sauce is ready, add the mozzarella which has been cut into fine strips. It will start to melt most immediately so it should be added to the sauce just before the pasta is drained. Pour the sauce over the pasta, stir well and serve.
The freshly grated Parmesan is served separately.

Rigatoni al Forno con Salsa Aurora

Baked Rigatoni with Aurora Sauce

'Rosy-fingered Dawn', beloved of the Latin poets, gives her name to this recipe.

500 g/1 lb rigatoni or other short pasta
100 g/4 oz (1 stick) butter
90 g/3½ oz (4½ tbsp) flour
750 ml/1¼ pints (3 cups) milk
250 ml/8 fl oz tomato sauce (see recipe page 36)
salt and black pepper
125 g/4 oz (1½ cups) freshly grated Parmesan cheese
120 ml/8 tbsp toasted breadcrumbs

Make a bechamel sauce using 80 g/3 oz (6 tbsp) butter, the flour and the milk.
Stir in the tomato sauce. Check for seasoning and add salt and freshly ground
pepper if needed.
Cook the pasta for half the time given in the packet directions, drain and mix well
with the sauce and half the freshly grated cheese. Turn into a buttered oven dish and
cover with the rest of the grated cheese mixed with the breadcrumbs.
Dot with the remaining butter.
Bake in a hot oven for 10 minutes. If a browner crust is desired, place under a hot
grill (broiler) for a few minutes.

Penne al Forno con Pomodoro e Mozzarella

Baked Penne with Tomato and Cheese

500 g/1 lb penne or other short pasta
tomato sauce (full quantity of recipe page 36)
50 g/2 oz (generous ½ cup) freshly grated
Parmesan cheese
300 g/10 oz mozzarella cheese
120 ml/8 tbsp toasted breadcrumbs

Cook the pasta for half the time given in the packet directions and drain.
Put 120 ml/4 fl oz of the tomato sauce on one side and mix the rest with the pasta.
Add one-third of the freshly grated Parmesan cheese.
Butter an oven dish and put in half the pasta. Cover with thin slices of mozzarella,
the reserved tomato sauce and half the remaining Parmesan. Add the rest of the
pasta and cover with the remaining Parmesan mixed with the breadcrumbs.
Bake in a hot oven 220°C/425°F/Mark 7 for 20 minutes.

Courgettes
Zucchine

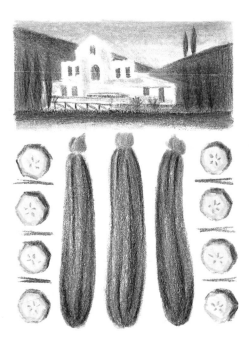

*T*welve kilometres from Sorrento along a road winding past apricot-coloured houses and banks of bougainvillaea and hibiscus, a road with a spectacular close-up view of the island of Capri, we come to the small fishing village of Marina di Cantone. The last nine kilometres of the precipitous road were finished only in 1960, and before this enthusiasts used to scramble down on foot, lured on by thoughts of the local pasta speciality, Spaghetti Maria Grazia, made with slivers of courgettes and cheese.

The first dish (over page) comes from the 'Maria Grazia' trattoria which has been owned for generations by the Mellino family. From the outside, it looks a little like a simple Greek taverna with its bright blue doors, pink-washed steps and white walls, and this impression is enhanced by the small white church which is the top floor of the trattoria. However, the art of combining the spiritual and temporal, illustrated by the pink trattoria tablecloths drying on the balcony next to the small church bell tower, is wholly Italian.

The simple, functional terrace where swim-suited guests eat within a few feet of the sea, is open only at lunchtime, but the fame of the pasta speciality has attracted a sophisticated clientele, many of whom arrive by yacht or even small boats from Positano and other ports along the craggy Amalfi coast.

Spaghetti Maria Grazia

500 g/1 lb spaghetti
2 kg/4 lb courgettes (zucchine)
oil for deep frying
salt and black pepper
150 g/5 oz (scant 2 cups) freshly grated cheese,
    half Parmesan and half pecorino romano
100 g/4 oz (1 stick) butter
a few basil leaves, if available

Choose small, tender courgettes and slice them finely in rounds without removing the skin. Heat a large quantity of oil and deep fry the courgettes until they are a deep golden brown and have become somewhat crumpled. Remove from the pan, but allow them to retain a little oil. (This can be done well in advance).
Cook the spaghetti in a large pan of boiling salted water, following the packet directions very carefully to make sure you do not overcook the pasta.
While the pasta is cooking, grate the cheese and gently warm the cooked courgettes in a pan. Divide the butter into small pieces and place in the serving bowl.
Drain the spaghetti when cooked, reserving 30-45 ml/2-3 tbsp of the water for the sauce. Gradually add the drained pasta to the butter in the serving bowl and add the reserved pasta water. It helps at this stage if there is someone to help with adding the pasta since the spaghetti should be stirred all the time to melt the butter and coat every strand.
Now add the grated cheese and stir again until all the cheese has melted and a thick yellow cream is clinging to the spaghetti. Stir in the courgettes and mix very thoroughly to ensure an even distribution. Add freshly ground black pepper to taste and basil leaves if available. Stir once more and serve immediately.

Spaghetti con Zucchine
Spaghetti with Courgettes

The traditional 'poor' version of spaghetti with courgettes, ideal for anyone avoiding animal fats, can be found throughout all the rural areas of Southern Italy where people have learned ways of making economical meals from their garden produce.

500 g/1 lb spaghetti
salt and black pepper
2 kg/4 lb tiny courgettes (zucchine)
150 ml/5 fl oz olive oil

Cook the pasta in a large pan of boiling, salted water, following the directions on the packet carefully to avoid overcooking.
While the pasta is cooking, slice the courgettes into thin rounds. Do not remove the skin. Fry them in hot olive oil until tender. When the pasta is cooked, drain it and stir in the courgettes and the olive oil in which they have been fried. Stir well, add black pepper to taste and serve. Cheese is not usually added to this dish.

Penne or Rigatoni con Zucchine

Penne with Courgettes, Mozzarella and Eggs

500 g/1 lb penne or rigatoni
1 kg/2 lb courgettes (zucchine)
150 ml/5 fl oz olive oil
salt and black pepper
50 g/2 oz (generous ½ cup) freshly grated
    Parmesan cheese
250 g/8 oz mozzarella cheese
2 eggs

Cut the courgettes into thin rounds, without peeling them and fry lightly in olive oil. The courgette slices should be just tender and bright green, so take care not to overcook them. When they are ready salt them and keep warm. Keep the olive oil to add to the final dish.
Grate the Parmesan cheese and cut the mozzarrella into small cubes. Cook the pasta following the packet directions very carefully to avoid overcooking. Beat the two eggs together. Immediately the pasta is cooked, drain it and pour while still steaming hot into the heated serving bowl. Add the cubed mozzarella and stir swiftly so that the hot pasta starts to melt the cheese. Now add the eggs, courgettes and reheated olive oil, stirring quickly to set the eggs. Add the Parmesan cheese and freshly ground black pepper to taste. Stir thoroughly and serve at once.

Pasticcio di Maccheroni con le Zucchine

Baked Pasta with Courgettes

500 g/1 lb short pasta such as farfalle, or tortiglione
1 kilo/2 lb courgettes
tomato sauce (full quantity of recipe page 36)
olive oil, approx 200 ml/7 fl oz
50 g/2 oz butter
300 g/10 oz mozzarella cheese

Cut the courgettes into thickish rounds, without peeling, and fry them lightly in olive oil. In a separate pan make the tomato sauce.
Cook the pasta in abundant boiling salted water, for half the time stated on the packet. Drain the pasta, add a knob of butter and mix well.
Butter a deep oven-proof serving dish and spread a thin layer of pasta at the bottom, then a layer of courgette slices, and cover these with thin slicces of mozzarella. Repeat these layers until you have used up all your ingredients, finishing with a layer of mozzarella. Dot the top with butter and bake in a hot oven, 220°C/425°F/Mark 7 for 20 minutes until melted and golden brown. Serve hot.

Spinach
Spinaci

*W*ashing fresh spinach has always been a rather tedious procedure, but it is now possible to buy bags of pre-washed spinach. In Italy it is usually washed in front of you if the market fountain is near enough, or else the stall lady – always the boss – orders her husband off to wash it for her!

Spinach plays three supporting roles with pasta: added to the fresh pasta dough to give it a green colour; mixed with ricotta cheese to make a delicate filling for stuffed pasta; or used to make subtle, light sauces for cooked pasta.

Linguine con Salsa di Spinaci
Linguine with Spinach

500 g/1 lb linguine or spaghetti
800 g/1½ lb fresh spinach leaves
60 g/2 oz (4 tbsp) butter
60 g/2 oz (¼ cup) flour
500 ml/16 fl oz milk
salt and black pepper
grated nutmeg
40 g/1½ oz (½ cup) freshly grated Parmesan cheese

Wash the spinach. Put a generous handful on one side and cook the rest very quickly in a covered saucepan. It will take about 5 minutes. Do not add any water, since the spinach will cook in the water remaining on the leaves after washing. Drain the spinach well, keeping the liquid to use later. Chop the spinach very finely and keep warm.

Make a bechamel sauce using the butter, flour and milk, then dilute with the reserved spinach liquid. Check for seasoning and add a little grated nutmeg.

Cook the pasta, following the packet directions very carefully. Add the cooked chopped spinach to the bechamel sauce and at the very last minute add the finely chopped raw spinach. This will make the sauce a more attractive green and improve the flavour. Pour onto the drained pasta, mix well and serve at once. Freshly grated Parmesan cheese can be served separately, if desired.

Tagliatelle al Mascarpone e Spinaci
Tagliatelle with Mascarpone and Spinach

500 g/1 lb tagliatelle
20 g/¾ oz (1½ tbsp) butter
1 clove garlic
300 g/10 oz fresh spinach leaves
150 ml/¼ pint double cream (⅔ cup heavy cream)
150 g/5 oz (about ⅔ cup) mascarpone cream cheese
a little chicken stock
salt and black pepper

Melt the butter and add the garlic, whole, allowing it to turn golden brown. Add the finely chopped spinach and cook over a low heat until tender. In a separate pan, put the cream and mascarpone, add a little stock to dilute and pepper to taste. Leave to simmer gently for a few minutes.
Cook the pasta, following the packet directions very carefully to avoid overcooking. Remove the garlic from the spinach. Drain the pasta, turn into a warm serving bowl and add first the cream sauce and then the spinach. Stir well and serve at once.

Pasticcio di Maccheroni con Salsa Verde
Baked Pasta Shells with a Green Sauce

500 g/1 lb conchiglie
1 kg/2 lb fresh spinach leaves
100 g/4 oz (1 stick) butter
250 ml/8 fl oz chicken stock
salt and black pepper
100 g/4 oz (1¼ cups) freshly grated Parmesan cheese
120 ml/8 tbsp toasted breadcrumbs

Wash the spinach and cook very quickly in a covered saucepan. It will take about 5 minutes. Do not add any water, since the spinach will cook in the water remaining on the leaves after washing. Drain well and chop the spinach finely. Melt 20 g/¾ oz (1½ tbsp) butter in a pan and add the chopped cooked spinach. Stir for about 5 minutes, then add the stock. Boil fiercely to reduce the sauce, then add seasoning to taste and 80 g/3 oz (1 cup) freshly grated cheese. You should now have a thick, creamy sauce.
Cook the pasta for 5 minutes less than stated in the instructions on the packet. Drain and toss in 60 g/2½ oz (5 tbsp) melted butter. Butter a deep oven dish and make alternate layers of pasta and green sauce, finishing with a pasta layer. Cover with the toasted crumbs mixed with the remaining cheese. Dot with the rest of the butter and add pepper to taste. Bake in a hot oven, 220°C/425°F/Mark 7, for 10 minutes, finishing under hot grill (broiler) if necessary.

Cauliflower
Cavolfiore

*I*n Italian markets it is possible to find both the round white cauliflower and the pointed green-flowered variety. They can both be used to make interesting sauces for pasta. The recipes given for broccoli and turnip tops can be made very successfully with cauliflower (see page 65) Here are two additional recipes, including a Sicilian version using nuts and raisins. Many vegetable sauces have the addition of nuts and raisins in Sicily, due to centuries of Arab influence.

Pasta 'chi Vrocculi Arriminati'
Rigatoni with Sicilian Cauliflower sauce

500 g/1 lb rigatoni
1 cauliflower
salt
30 ml/2 tbsp olive oil
1 onion
1 tsp saffron filaments or ¼ tsp powder dissolved
   in a little warm water
3 anchovy fillets
50 g/2 oz (⅓ cup) seedless raisins
50 g/2 oz (½-⅔ cup) pine nuts or chopped blanched
   almonds
50 g/2 oz (¾ cup) freshly grated pecorino romano or
   Parmesan cheese
4 basil leaves, if available

Wash the cauliflower, remove the coarse leaves and cook whole in boiling salted water. Do not overcook. While it is still firm, remove from the water with a slotted spoon; reserve the water.

In a large pan, heat half the oil and add the finely chopped onion. When it begins to turn colour, add the saffron which has been dissolved in a little warm water. Cover and cook for 10 minutes.

Divide the cauliflower into florets and add to the onion. Heat the rest of the oil in a small pan and cook the chopped anchovies until they have almost melted. Add to the cauliflower together with the raisins and nuts. Stir well and leave, covered, off the heat.

Add more boiling water and salt to the cauliflower water so that you have enough water to cook the pasta. Follow the packet directions carefully to avoid overcooking. Drain the pasta and stir in the cauliflower sauce. Add the freshly grated cheese and chopped basil. Mix well and serve.

Penne al Cavolfiore
Penne with Cauliflower

500 g/1 lb penne or other short pasta
20 ml/1½ tbsp olive oil
2 cloves garlic
1 small chilli
1 cauliflower
230 g/8 oz tin Italian plum tomatoes
250 ml/8 fl oz chicken stock
200 ml/⅓ pint double cream (1 cup heavy cream)

Heat the oil and add the chopped garlic and the whole or chopped chilli pepper.
Cook for 10 minutes, then add the cauliflower divided into florets. After another
5 minutes cooking, and the chopped tomatoes with their juice. Cook gently for
10 minutes, then add the stock.
Leave to simmer while you cook the pasta following the packet directions very
carefully to avoid overcooking.
Add the cream to the cauliflower mixture and remove the chilli if whole.
Squash the cauliflower with a potato masher. Drain the pasta and stir in the sauce.
Serve at once.

Black Olives
Olive Nere

*T*he tradition of using olives to make sauces is thought to go back to ancient Roman times. No one knows whether it was the oil or the whole fruit that was first used to flavour other food. This Ligurian sauce relies on olives, olive oil and garlic to produce a tasty pastry dish.

Linguine alle Olive
Linguine with Black Olives

500 g/1 lb linguine or spaghetti
2 cloves garlic
200 g/7 oz pitted black olives
50 ml/3½ tbsp olive oil
parsley salt

Chop the garlic and olives and leave to macerate in half the olive oil for several hours, overnight if possible. The olives give out more liquid this way.
Cook the pasta, following packet directions carefully to avoid over-cooking. While the pasta is cooking heat the rest of the oil and pour in the olives. Add chopped parsley and salt to taste. Leave to simmer gently.
Drain the pasta and stir in the olive sauce. Cheese is not usually served with this recipe.

Penne alle Olive
Penne with Olive and Tomato Sauce

The large black olives from Gaeta, the seaside town just north of Naples, are usually used for this recipe, but any fleshy black olive may be used just as well.

500 g/1 lb penne or other short pasta
30 ml/2 tbsp olive oil
2 cloves garlic
1 small chilli pepper or 5 ml/1 tsp dried chilli pepper
   flakes
800 g/28 oz tinned Italian plum tomatoes
200 g/7 oz large black olives
parsley salt

Heat the oil and fry the chopped garlic and chilli until the garlic turns golden brown. Now add the tomatoes with their juice and cook for 20 minutes. Add the chopped, pitted black olives and salt to taste.
Cook the pasta, following the packet directions carefully to avoid over-cooking. Drain, turn into a heated serving dish and stir in the sauce. Sprinkle the chopped parsley on top.

Rocket
Rughetta or Rucola

*I*n Italy, rocket can be found in every market in two versions – wild and cultivated. The wild *rughetta* has spiky leaves and a strong flavour, while the cultivated *rughetta* has larger leaves and a milder taste. It is used in appetizers, pasta dishes, meat dishes and salads.

If there is any *rughetta* and fresh Parmesan cheese left over after making pasta sauce, it is simple to produce a delicious side dish. Wash and dry the rocket leaves, dress with a little olive oil and then cover with fine shavings of Parmesan cheese.

Spaghetti alla Rughetta
Spaghetti with Rocket

500 g/1 lb spaghetti
60 ml/4 tbsp olive oil
4 cloves garlic
1 or 2 small chilli peppers
100 g/4 oz rocket leaves

Cook the pasta, following the packet directions carefully to avoid overcooking. While the pasta is cooking heat the oil and gently fry the chopped garlic and chilli pepper. During the last 5 minutes of the pasta cooking, throw the rocket in with the pasta. Drain well, and stir in the garlic, chilli and the hot oil. Serve at once.

Spaghetti con Pomodori e Rughetta
Spaghetti with Fresh Tomatoes and Rocket

In summer, if you can get fresh plum tomatoes, you can make this unusual cold sauce.

500 g/1 lb spaghetti
300 g/10 oz red ripe plum tomatoes
4 cloves garlic
50 g/2 oz rocket (about ⅓ cup chopped)
20 ml/1½ tbsp olive oil
salt and black pepper

Skin the tomatoes by first plunging them into boiling water for a few minutes. Chop finely and place in a large bowl together with the finely chopped garlic and coarsely chopped rocket. Add the olive oil and salt and pepper to taste and leave for at least 2 hours.
Cook the pasta as usual, drain and stir in the sauce.

Onions
Cipolle

Onions are used in conjunction with other ingredients in many pasta sauces but they also make a delicious sauce by themselves.

Tagliatelle con Cipolle
Tagliatelle with Onion Sauce

500 g/1 lb tagliatelle
100 g/4 oz (1 stick) butter
500 g/1 lb onions
chicken stock
200 ml/7 fl oz double (heavy) cream
salt and black pepper
grated nutmeg

Melt the butter and cook the thinly sliced onions in a covered pan over a low heat until they are soft. Do not let them turn brown. Cover with chicken stock and simmer with the lid on for another 25 minutes. Purée the cooked onions and add the cream and salt, pepper and nutmeg to taste. Keep warm.

Cook the pasta, following the packet directions carefully to avoid over-cooking. Drain the pasta, pour into a heated serving bowl and stir in the sauce. Freshly grated Parmesan cheese may be served separately.

An even simpler version of this sauce can be made by omitting the cream and adding anchovies. The peeled onions are left under cold running water for an hour. They are then sliced and cooked as in the previous recipe but the butter is replaced by 50 ml/3 tablespoons of olive oil. Six finely chopped anchovy fillets are cooked slowly in the olive oil. While the pasta is cooking the anchovies are added to the onions. In this recipe spaghetti or bucatini are usually used. When the pasta is drained it is tossed in 50 grams (2 oz) of freshly grated Parmesan cheese, then the sauce is stirred thoroughly into the pasta.

For another powerful onion sauce see also
Rigatoni alla Genovese, (p.110).

Sweet Peppers
Peperoni

The rather sweet, large, shiny red and yellow peppers are used in preference to green in pasta sauces.

In Italy, peppers are usually skinned because the skin is thought to be indigestible and bitter in taste. Place the peppers under a very hot grill (broiler) and turn them until all the skin is uniformly black. The skin can then be peeled off quite easily and the pepper itself remains firm. The pepper can also be skinned after being roasted in a hot oven (see page 22).

This pasta recipe was first cooked for me in Acqua Viva in Castro, Puglia. The Salento peninsula seems to produce very individual recipes and the smell of this little-known pepper sauce conjures up visions for me of the small natural harbour, the rocky coastline and the winding road leading up to the castle and fortified old town of Castro, believed to be the Castrum Minervae of Virgil's *Aeneid*.

Penne con Peperoni
Quills with Sweet Pepper Sauce

500 g/1 lb penne or other short pasta
1 kg/2 lb sweet red and yellow peppers
60 ml/4 tbsp olive oil
4 cloves garlic
salt
parsley

Remove the seeds and fibres from the peppers and cut them into strips about the same size as the pasta. Heat the oil, add the chopped garlic and when it begins to run colour add the peppers. Cover and cook gently for 10 minutes. Remove the lid and turn up the heat. Cook for another 5 minutes. Add salt to taste.
Cook the pasta, following packet directions carefully to avoid over-cooking. Drain, turn into a heated serving bowl and stir in the pepper mixture and the chopped parsley. Serve at once.

Peperoni Ripieni di Pasta
Sweet Peppers with Pasta Stuffing

250 g/8 oz small pasta
6 large equal-sized sweet peppers
salt and black pepper
15 ml/1 tbsp olive oil
200 g/7 oz black olives
chopped parsley
1 clove garlic
4 anchovy fillets
1 teaspoon capers
200 g/7 oz mozzarella cheese

Cut the tops off the peppers and remove the seeds, always being careful not to pierce the peppers. Sprinkle the inside with salt, pepper and a little oil. Pit the olives and chop them together with the parsley, garlic, anchovies and capers. Cut the mozzarella into small cubes.
Cook the pasta for half the time stated in the directions on the packet.
Drain and stir in the chopped ingredients and cheese. Fill the peppers with this mixture. Place them on a greased baking tray and cook in a moderately hot oven, 200°C/400°F/Mark 6, for 35 minutes. If, during the cooking period, the peppers appear to be browning too quickly, cover them with a sheet of foil.

Linguine con Peperoni
Linguine with Sweet Pepper

500 g/1 lb linguine or spaghetti
40 ml/2½ tbsp olive oil
3 cloves garlic
1 onion
6 large sweet red and yellow peppers
salt

Heat the oil and add the roughly chopped garlic and onion. Remove the seeds and coarse fibres from the peppers, roughly chop them and add to the onions and garlic. Add a little salt and stew in a covered pan over a low heat for 2 hours. (I prefer to do this in an earthenware pot in the oven.) The peppers will produce their own liquid and practically melt into the sauce.
Pass the mixture through a seive or the fine blade of a food mill. (A blender or processor does not produce the same effect.) Keep the sauce warm.
Cook the pasta, following packet directions very carefully to avoid over-cooking.
Drain and turn into a heated serving bowl. Stir in the sauce and serve at once.
A similar sauce can be made using 2 red, 2 yellow and 2 green peppers, and half the quantity of oil. After the peppers are passed through the food mill, a little cream is stirred into the sauce before it is added to the pasta.

Courgette Flowers
Courgette Flowers

Courgette and other squash flowers are rarely seen for sale outside Italy. But there these spectacular yellow flowers are sold in bunches and are eaten either stuffed with anchovies and mozzarella cheese, dipped in batter and fried, or used to make deliciously different pasta sauces.

Here are two versions for keen gardeners who grow their own. The flowers need to be cooked when they are very fresh. The stalk, hairy calyx and stamens are removed and the flower is wiped with a moist kitchen towel. It is too delicate to be washed in water.

Spaghetti ai Fiori di Zucca
Spaghetti with Courgette Flowers

500 g/1 lb spaghetti
60 ml/4 tbsp olive oil
3 cloves garlic
¼ small chilli pepper, or 2.5 ml/½ tsp dried pepper flakes
8 courgette or marrow (squash) flowers

Heat the oil and fry the chopped garlic and chilli pepper. Add the chopped courgette flowers and stir for 5 minutes, then keep warm. Cook the spaghetti carefully to avoid overcooking. Just before draining, re-heat the sauce so that it is very hot. Drain the pasta, pour over the sauce, stir quickly to coat every strand with oil and serve.

Vermicelli Abruzzesi
Pasta and Courgette Flowers from Abruzzi

This recipe comes from the Abruzzi region in the middle of Italy, the centre of the saffron industry. It takes 130,000 crocus flowers to produce one kilo of saffron, which explains the high cost.

500 g/1 lb vermicelli or spaghetti
30 ml/1 tbsp olive oil
1 onion
5 ml/1 tsp saffron filaments or ¼ teaspoon powder
    dissolved in a little hot stock
60 ml/4 tbsp chopped parsley
8 courgette or marrow (squash) flowers
200 ml/⅓ pint (1 cup) stock
1 egg yolk
40 g/1½ oz (½ cup) freshly grated Parmesan
salt and black pepper

Heat the oil and fry the chopped onion gently until soft. Add the saffron dissolved in the hot stock, the parsley and the chopped courgette flowers. Cook for 10 minutes. Process or blend with the stock, then return to the pan to keep warm. Cook the pasta, following the packet directions carefully to avoid overcooking. Remove the sauce from the heat and add the egg yolk, freshly grated cheese and seasoning to taste. Stir well. Drain the pasta, pour on the sauce, mix thoroughly and serve.

Asparagus
Asparagi

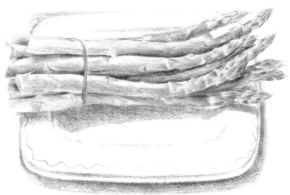

Green asparagus makes a deliciously different sauce to go with fresh pasta or dried pasta made with egg. Now that the short, spring season is extended with imports, asparagus recipes are worth collecting.

Pasta al Forno con Asparagi
Baked Pasta with Asparagus

400 g/14 oz penne or other short pasta
1 kg/2 lb asparagus
120 g/4 oz (1 stick) butter
a little chicken stock
salt and black pepper
300 g/10 oz (about 1½ cups) ricotta or similar
 curd cheese
15 ml/1 tbsp olive oil
125 g/4 oz (1¼ cups) freshly grated Parmesan cheese
3 eggs

Wash the asparagus, remove any tough stalks and cut into short lengths.
Melt 40 g/1½ oz (3 tbsp) butter in a pan and cook the asparagus over a low heat for about 20 minutes. Every so often, add a little stock to keep moist. When the asparagus is cooked, season to taste.
While the asparagus is cooking, process the ricotta cheese with the oil. Cook the pasta for half the time stated on the packet. Drain and immediately toss in the remaining butter and half the freshly grated cheese.
Butter a deep oven dish. Make a thin layer of pasta, then one of asparagus, then one of pasta again and then one of ricotta. Repeat, finishing with a layer of pasta.
Beat together the eggs and the remaining cheese and pour over the top. Sprinkle with black pepper. Bake in a medium oven, 180°C/350°F/Mark 4, for 20 minutes.

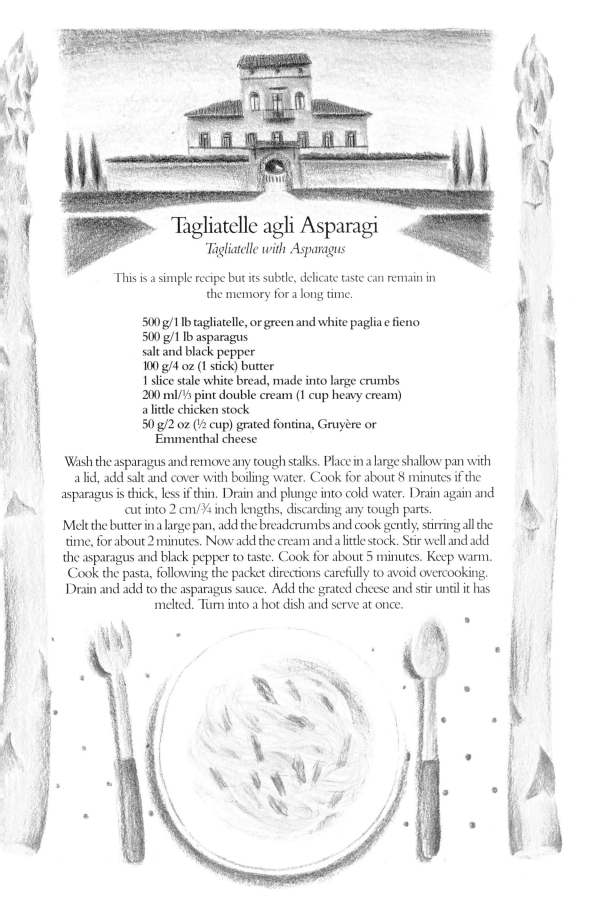

Tagliatelle agli Asparagi
Tagliatelle with Asparagus

This is a simple recipe but its subtle, delicate taste can remain in
the memory for a long time.

500 g/1 lb tagliatelle, or green and white paglia e fieno
500 g/1 lb asparagus
salt and black pepper
100 g/4 oz (1 stick) butter
1 slice stale white bread, made into large crumbs
200 ml/⅓ pint double cream (1 cup heavy cream)
a little chicken stock
50 g/2 oz (½ cup) grated fontina, Gruyère or
  Emmenthal cheese

Wash the asparagus and remove any tough stalks. Place in a large shallow pan with
a lid, add salt and cover with boiling water. Cook for about 8 minutes if the
asparagus is thick, less if thin. Drain and plunge into cold water. Drain again and
cut into 2 cm/¾ inch lengths, discarding any tough parts.
Melt the butter in a large pan, add the breadcrumbs and cook gently, stirring all the
time, for about 2 minutes. Now add the cream and a little stock. Stir well and add
the asparagus and black pepper to taste. Cook for about 5 minutes. Keep warm.
Cook the pasta, following the packet directions carefully to avoid overcooking.
Drain and add to the asparagus sauce. Add the grated cheese and stir until it has
melted. Turn into a hot dish and serve at once.

Green Vegetables
La Verdura

*T*here are many delicious sauces made using a mixture of green vegetables. Here are two of them. La Primavera is an extravagant recipe because it needs fresh young vegetables, at a time when they are still comparatively expensive. Each vegetable has to be prepared separately to guarantee its perfection. However, it makes a spectacular first course for a spring dinner party and the vegetables can be prepared a little in advance.

Pasta alla Primavera
Spring Pasta

500 g/1 lb tagliolini (tagliarini), green if available
12 spears tender young asparagus
200 g/7 oz (1½ cups) shelled fresh peas, the smaller
    the better
200 g/7 oz (1¼ cups) small shelled broad (fava) beans
    or fine green beans
salt and black pepper
30 g/1 oz (2 tbsp) butter
200 ml/⅓ pint double cream (1 cup heavy cream)
60 g/2½ oz (¾ cup) freshly grated Parmesan cheese

Cook each vegetable separately in a small quantity of boiling salted water. It is better to slightly under-cook because the vegetables must remain crisp and a good green colour. Drain and plunge immediately into cold water. Cut the asparagus (the tender part) into 2 cm/¾ inch lengths. Remove the outer skin of the shelled broad beans. If you are substituting green beans, cut them into small lengths.

Heat the water for the pasta. Melt the butter in a small pan and as you add the pasta to the water add the various green vegetables to the butter. Stir for 2 minutes, then add the cream and pepper to taste and heat gently.

Drain the pasta and turn into a warmed serving dish. Toss thoroughly with the freshly grated cheese, then add the vegetables and cream. Stir to distribute the vegetables evenly and serve at once.

Pasta con la Verdura
Pasta with Green Vegetables

This recipe can be made very successfully with any green vegetable you happen to have during the winter months. It is economical, very simple to prepare and one of my favourites.

500 g/1 lb tagliatelle, paglia e fieno or fresh
    wholewheat ribbon pasta
salt
3 medium-size potatoes
250 g/8 oz broccoli or cauliflower
4 small courgettes (zucchine) or green beans
500 g/1 lb fresh spinach leaves, or Chinese leaves
    (Nappa cabbage) or lettuce
30 g/1 oz (2 tbsp) butter
1 large onion
100 g/4 oz (1 cup) grated fontina or
    Emmenthal cheese

Bring a pan of salted water to the boil, large enough to take all the ingredients.
Add the potatoes, cut into pieces the size of a walnut, and cook for 10 minutes.
Then add the broccoli cut into thin spears, the small whole courgettes
and the spinach.
Meanwhile, in a small frying pan, melt the butter and add the finely chopped onion.
Cover and cook gently until soft.
Ten minutes after adding the last green vegetable to the pan, add the tagliatelle or
fresh pasta, both of which cook very quickly. Have a large ovenproof serving dish
ready and a hot oven (220°C/425°F/Mark 7).
Drain the pasta and green vegetables thoroughly in a very large sieve or colander.
Place half the pasta and vegetables in the serving dish. Add a layer of half the onions
and half the freshly grated cheese. Now add the rest of the pasta and vegetables and
the rest of the onions and cheese. Put in the oven, heat for 5 minutes, then serve.

Broccoli, Turnip Tops, Greens
Broccoli, Cime di Rape, Broccoletti

*P*uglia is one of the most interesting and least-known regions of Italy. Its remote position in the 'heel' helped it preserve its secrets, and the gaunt, ruined Saracen towers guarding the coastline remind us that this region was more vulnerable to approaches from the sea than from the land. The land, in fact, is very fertile: some of the best Italian wine and olive oil is produced in Puglia, and the region is famous for the excellence and variety of its green vegetables.

The most characteristic sauce of the region is made from green vegetables and a pasta unique to Puglia – orecchiette or 'little ears'. Originally the ears were always brown, made from wholewheat flour, but nowadays a white version is also made from more refined flour. The ears are made by hand and it is fascinating to see the speed with which the local women sculpt these ears from the fresh sheets of pasta.

Some fresh pasta shops outside Italy will make orecchiette to order, and it is possible to buy packets of dried orecchiette. If you do not find the right pasta shape you can use conchiglie, penne or rigatoni instead. It will not look as interesting but it will taste just as good. I have even used spaghetti at times and I must confess I like the way the greenery twists round the strings of spaghetti.

The traditional green vegetable to use with the following recipe is turnip tops. In Puglia the crop is sown for the tops, not the turnips. I have seen Pugliesi who have 'emigrated' to Rome or Milan returning North with carrier bags sprouting greenery. It is certainly true that the southern *cime di rape* have a distinctive, pungent flavour that is not found in the Rome vegetable. However, this recipe can be made very successfully using purple-flowering broccoli, calabrese broccoli or indeed any tender, young leafy green vegetable.

Orecchiette con Cime di Rape
Orecchiette with Turnip Tops

500 g/1 lb orecchiette or other short pasta
600 g/1¼ lb turnip tops, broccoli or tender spring
   (or other) greens
salt
60 ml/4 tbsp olive oil
5 cloves garlic
1 or 2 small chilli peppers or 10 ml/2 tsp dried
   crushed chillies (hot red pepper flakes)

Wash the greens and cut into long thin strips. If using broccoli, divide up the florets
and slice the stalks in half so that they cook more quickly. Discard the very thick
pieces of stalk. Heat a large pan of salted water and when it is boiling plunge in the
green vegetables. Do not overcook. They must remain crisp and a good vivid
green. Drain the greens but keep the water.
Bring the water back to the boil – check that there is sufficient for cooking the pasta,
adding more water if necessary. Cook the pasta, following the packet directions
carefully to avoid overcooking.
While the pasta is cooking, heat the olive oil in a large pan. Add the chopped garlic
and chilli pepper. (Add the chilli pepper whole for a less hot sauce.) Stir until the
garlic is golden brown. Do not allow it to get too dark.
When the pasta is almost ready, put the greens back into the pan with the pasta and
cook together for another 3 minutes. Drain carefully, shaking the sieve or colander
to remove any water trapped in the crevices of the pasta ears. Turn into a large,
warmed serving dish, stir well and add the very hot oil mixture. If the chilli pepper
is whole, remove it. Stir well and serve at once. Cheese is not served with this recipe.
Another version of this dish, also from Puglia, adds 6 anchovy fillets, rinsed and
finely chopped, to the garlic and chilli during the initial frying period.

Orecchiette con Broccoli e Pomodoro
Orecchiette with Broccoli and Tomatoes

500 g/1 lb orecchiette
600 g/1¼ lb broccoli
salt
tomato sauce (full quantity of recipe page 36)
80 g/3 oz (1 cup) freshly grated Parmesan cheese
parsley

Cook the broccoli and pasta as in the prevous recipe. Add the broccoli to the pasta
for the last 3 minutes cooking. Drain well and put in a hot serving dish. Stir well
and add the hot tomato sauce. Stir again, then add the freshly grated cheese.
Mix well together, sprinkle with chopped parsley and serve at once.

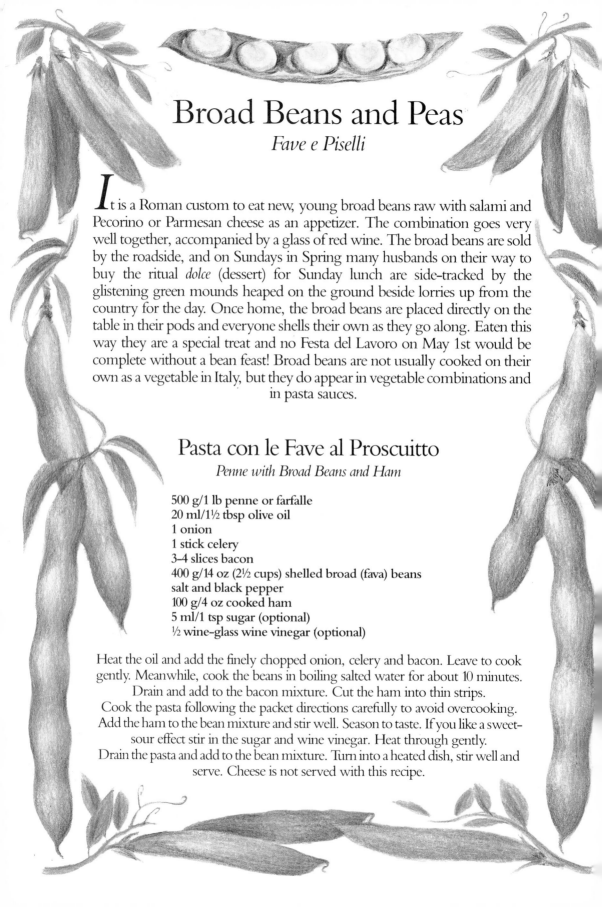

Broad Beans and Peas
Fave e Piselli

*I*t is a Roman custom to eat new, young broad beans raw with salami and Pecorino or Parmesan cheese as an appetizer. The combination goes very well together, accompanied by a glass of red wine. The broad beans are sold by the roadside, and on Sundays in Spring many husbands on their way to buy the ritual *dolce* (dessert) for Sunday lunch are side-tracked by the glistening green mounds heaped on the ground beside lorries up from the country for the day. Once home, the broad beans are placed directly on the table in their pods and everyone shells their own as they go along. Eaten this way they are a special treat and no Festa del Lavoro on May 1st would be complete without a bean feast! Broad beans are not usually cooked on their own as a vegetable in Italy, but they do appear in vegetable combinations and in pasta sauces.

Pasta con le Fave al Proscuitto
Penne with Broad Beans and Ham

500 g/1 lb penne or farfalle
20 ml/1½ tbsp olive oil
1 onion
1 stick celery
3-4 slices bacon
400 g/14 oz (2½ cups) shelled broad (fava) beans
salt and black pepper
100 g/4 oz cooked ham
5 ml/1 tsp sugar (optional)
½ wine-glass wine vinegar (optional)

Heat the oil and add the finely chopped onion, celery and bacon. Leave to cook gently. Meanwhile, cook the beans in boiling salted water for about 10 minutes. Drain and add to the bacon mixture. Cut the ham into thin strips.
Cook the pasta following the packet directions carefully to avoid overcooking.
Add the ham to the bean mixture and stir well. Season to taste. If you like a sweet-sour effect stir in the sugar and wine vinegar. Heat through gently.
Drain the pasta and add to the bean mixture. Turn into a heated dish, stir well and serve. Cheese is not served with this recipe.

Tagliolini e Piselli

Tagliolini with Fresh Peas

500 g/1 lb tagliolini (tagliarini) or small short pasta
600 g/1¼ lb (4 cups) shelled fresh peas
salt and black pepper
150 g/5 oz (1 stick & 2 tbsp) butter
1 onion
6 basil leaves, if available
100 g/4 oz (1¼ cups) freshly grated Parmesan cheese

Cook the peas in boiling salted water for 5 minutes, then drain, reserving
4 tablespoons of the cooking liquid, and plunge into cold water.
Melt the butter and add the finely chopped onion. Cook until soft but do not allow
to turn colour. Cook the pasta following the packet directions carefully to avoid
overcooking. In the last 5 minutes of the pasta cooking time, add the peas to the
butter and onions with the reserved pea liquid and season to taste.
Drain the pasta, stir in cheese and add the peas. Stir well. Add the chopped basil
and serve.

Pasta e Piselli con la Pancetta

Pasta with Peas and Bacon

500 g/1 lb penne or farfalle
20 ml/1½ tbsp olive oil
30 g/1 oz (2 tbsp) butter
300 g/10 oz (2 cups) chopped onion
150 g/5 oz bacon
600 g/1¼ lb (4 cups) shelled fresh or frozen peas
salt and black pepper
100 g/4 oz (1¼ cups) freshly grated Parmesan cheese

Heat the oil and butter in a large pan and add the chopped onion. Cook for about
5 minutes, then add the bacon cut into small cubes. When the bacon is nearly
cooked add the peas. Season to taste and leave to cook gently.
Cook the pasta for 5 minutes less than the time stated in the packet directions.
Drain and add to the pea mixture, together with 4 tablespoons of the pasta water.
Cover and cook for another 5 minutes. Do not drain. Serve the freshly grated
cheese separately.

Pumpkin
Zucca

*A*utumn is the time of the year for pumpkin pasta dishes. They can be made with the beautiful, golden Cinderella-type pumpkin or with slices of the more prosaic green squashes. The sauce here has a very delicate flavour and it is very important to use good quality, freshly-grated cheese. It is particularly delicious with fine, fresh pasta.

This recipe was given to me by Angelina Di Mambro of Ponte Milvio market in Rome. As she explained the recipe she cut up the pumpkin, leek and celery with lightning speed. She always chooses the most fragrant basil, the crispest rocket and the most beautiful vegetables for me, and takes a keen interest in remembering and explaining traditional recipes.

Tagliolini con la Zucca
Pumpkin Pasta

500 g/1 lb tagliolini (tagliarini) made with eggs,
    or fine fresh pasta
1.5 kg/3 lb piece of pumpkin
50 g/2 oz (4 tbsp) butter
1 leek
1 stick celery
chicken stock
salt and black pepper
grated nutmeg
150 ml/¼ pint double cream (⅔ cup heavy cream),
    or 125 g/4 oz fromage frais
70 g/3 oz (scant 1 cup) freshly grated Parmesan cheese

Melt half the butter and add the finely chopped leek and celery.
Peel the pumpkin and remove the seeds and any stringy fibres. Cut the pumpkin into thin slices.
Add to the leek and celery and stir for a few minutes. Now add a little stock and cover. Cook for about 20 minutes, adding more stock from time to time if necessary to keep moist. Check the seasoning and add salt, freshly ground black pepper and nutmeg to taste. Process the sauce in a blender or food processor.
Return to the pan and keep warm.
Cook the pasta carefully and avoid overcooking. Fresh pasta will only need a few minutes, so add the cream to the sauce as soon as you have thrown the pasta into the boiling water. Drain the pasta and place in a heated dish. Stir in the freshly grated cheese and then the pumpkin sauce. Mix well, add the rest of the butter and serve at once.

Chick Peas

Ceci

One of the earliest recorded pasta sauces, and certainly one that has a most interesting combination of textures uses plump, firm chick peas combined with soft, boiled pasta and crisp, crunchy pasta that has been fried in olive oil. This contrasting soft and crisp dish is a speciality of Lecce and the Salento Peninsula in the region of Puglia in the southern heel of Italy; it is virtually unknown elsewhere.

This unusual method of frying the dry pasta does not appear in any other existing recipe but at one time it seems to have been common practice. In the fifteenth century, a prelate in Florence criticized his congregation's over-elaborate cuisine by upbraiding them: "It is not enough for you to eat your pasta fried, you think you must add garlic too!"

The frying technique is believed to have developed from the earlier method of rolling out the flour and water paste, baking it on a large, flat stone and cutting the resulting crisp disc into long strips to be added to the other ingredients. The ancient Romans discovered the chick pea recipe when they travelled south to Brindisi on their way to Greece, and the Roman poet, Horace, in one of his Satires, writes of the delightful prospect of a plate of pasta and chick peas awaiting him at home: *"Inde domum me – ad porri et ciceris refero laganique catinum."*

The dish continued to be enjoyed during the following centuries and became adapted to the dry pasta introduced by the Arabs. It lost its Latin name *'laganelle'* and became *'tria'* from the Arabic *'itrya'* meaning dry pasta with a hole. Today this dish is still called *'ciceri e tria'* – chick peas and pasta.

After all these hundreds of years the recipe is still a winner. The subtle combination of flavours and textures makes it an interesting, unusual dish. And because of the high-fibre and protein contents of both the chick peas and pasta the dish appeals to all health-conscious cooks. It is also very economical, and if the dried chick peas are replaced by tinned chick peas, a substantial meal can be produced from the store cupboard in twenty minutes.

Ideally, this recipe is best made with dried ribbon-type pasta that does not contain eggs. However, if this is unobtainable it can be made very successfully with dried *tagliatelle* containing eggs. Green and white pasta could also be used, and adds to the colourful appearance of the final dish. Fresh pasta is not suitable for this recipe. Use good quality olive oil to fry the pasta as this contributes to the final flavour.

Ciceri e Tria
Chick Peas and Pasta

300 g/10 oz tagliatelle
300 g/10 oz dried chick peas,
   or 2 425 g/15 oz tins chick peas
5 ml/1 tsp bicarbonate of soda
salt and freshly ground black pepper
1 bay leaf
1 clove garlic
1 onion
1 carrot
1 stick celery
fresh parsley
230 g/8 oz tin Italian plum tomatoes
olive oil

Wash the dried chick peas very thoroughly and put them in a bowl with plenty of tepid water. Add the bicarbonate of soda and 5 ml/1 tsp salt to the water.
Soak for at least 12 hours.
Drain the chick peas and put them to boil in plenty of fresh water, with the bay leaf, for 1 hour.
Meanwhile, finely chop the garlic, onion, carrot, celery and parsley together.
A food processor is ideal for this.
When the chick peas have cooked for 1 hour, drain them and return to the pan. Add the chopped vegetables and tomatoes with their juice. Cover with boiling water and cook for another hour, being very careful not to let the pan boil dry. If you are using tinned chick peas, drain them and cook the chopped vegetables in the liquid. Only add the chick peas themselves at the last moment to heat them gently.
When the chick peas are ready, boil a large quantity of water, add salt and then add half the quantity of pasta. Cook, following the directions on the packet very carefully so that you do not overcook the pasta. Break the remaining uncooked pasta into short pieces.
When the boiled pasta is nearly ready, heat some olive oil in a frying pan. Drain the boiled pasta, turn it into a large heated serving bowl, preferably earthenware, and add the cooked chick peas, which should have absorbed most of the water and be in a thick, rich sauce. Stir well.
Now, at the last possible moment, fry the short lengths of pasta in the hot oil, stirring all the time with a wooden spoon. It will only take a few minutes for the pasta to swell, crisp and turn golden brown. Add this fried pasta and the olive oil to the serving bowl, mix well and serve immediately while the fried pasta is still very crunchy.

Lampe e Tuone
Lightning and Thunder

The name doubtless comes from the effect of the hot chilli and chick peas on the digestion.

> 400 g/14 oz tagliatelle
> 300 g/10 oz dried chick peas,
>   or, 2 425 g/15 oz tins chick peas
> 5 ml/1 tsp bicarbonate of soda
> salt
> 90 ml/6 tbsp olive oil
> 2 cloves garlic
> 15 ml/1 tbsp fresh parsley
> 5 ml/1 tsp dried oregano
> ½ small hot chilli, seeded,
>   or 5 ml/1 tsp dried crushed chillies

Soak the chick peas as in the previous recipe, then drain and put in a saucepan with the oil and chopped garlic. Add 1 litre/1¾ pints (1 quart) of boiling water but no salt at this stage. Cook for about 2 hours until the chick peas are tender, taking care not to let them boil dry. Add more boiling water if necessary.
When these chick peas are just about ready (or if you are starting with tinned chick peas), add the chopped parsley, oregano, chilli and salt to taste.
Transfer the chick peas to a larger saucepan. Add 2 litres/3½ pints (2 quarts) of boiling water and when the mixture comes back to the boil add the pasta.
Cook until the pasta is ready, drain and serve immediately.

Pasta e Ceci
Chick Pea and Pasta Broth

> 250 g/8 oz short pasta such as ditalini, or long pasta
>   broken into short lengths
> 300 g/10 oz dried chick peas
> 5 ml/1 tsp bicarbonate of soda
> salt and freshly ground black pepper
> 15 to 30 ml/1 to 2 tbsp olive oil
> 4 rashers streaky bacon, cut into strips
> 2 cloves garlic
> 230 g/8 oz tin Italian plum tomatoes
> 2 bay leaves

Soak the dried chick peas as before, then drain and put in a saucepan with 2.5 litres/4 pints (2½ quarts) warm water.
In 1 spoonful of olive oil, gently fry the bacon strips and chopped garlic, then add the chopped tinned tomatoes and bay leaves. Add this mixture to the chick peas.
Cook slowly for about 2½ hours. Discard the bay leaves.
Purée half the chick pea mixture, then return to the remaining mixture in the saucepan. Bring back to the boil and add the pasta. Cook for a further 15 minutes.
Add salt and pepper to taste and serve. Most Italians also add a spoonful of 'uncooked' olive oil at the table.

Continental or European Lentils
Lenticchie

*T*hese greeny brown lentils keep their shape when they are cooked and go very well with pasta. They make a tasty nutritious cold-weather dish.

Pasta e Lenticchie
Small Pasta and Lentil Broth

400 g/14 oz small pasta such as ditalini
300 g/10 oz (1⅔ cups) green lentils
20 ml/2 tbsp olive oil
1 onion
1 stick celery
2 cloves garlic
1 small chilli pepper
500 ml/16 fl oz chicken stock
salt and black pepper

Lentils must first be washed under running water and any small stones or pieces of stalk removed. Then they must be soaked. If you have plenty of time, cover the lentils with twice their volume of cold water and leave 12 hours. If you are in a hurry, you can speed up the process by putting them in a pan and covering with cold water. Bring to the boil and cook for 5 minutes. Remove from the heat and leave to soak, covered, for 1 hour.
Cook the drained lentils in cold unsalted water for 30 minutes. Heat the oil and gently fry the chopped vegetables and chilli pepper for about 5 minutes. Drain the lentils, return to the pan and add the hot stock and cooked vegetables. Cook for another 20 minutes, covered, on a low heat.
Now remove the lid and add the pasta. It should take about 10 minutes to cook. Have boiling water ready to add if the mixture becomes too dry. When ready it should be a thick broth, in which, according to Italian tradition, one should be able to stand a spoon. Add salt to taste. Do not drain. Serve at once.
In the Sicilian version of this dish the lentils are cooked then processed to make a thick purée. The small pasta is cooked and drained then mixed with the puréed lentils, black pepper and freshly grated Parmesan cheese.

Dried Beans
Fagioli

*I*n Italy it is possible to buy beans that have been dried in their pods. The pods are a colourful combination of scarlet and cream streaks. These beans do not need soaking. However, during the winter dried beans as we know them are used. These can be bought by weight in the local market. Various qualities are displayed in their sacks and the careful shopper makes sure to choose fresh shiny beans. Those most commonly used for pasta are cannellini or borlotti.

Bucatini ai Fagioli
Bucatini with Beans

500 g/1 lb bucatini or spaghetti
150 g/5 oz (¾ cup) dried beans
60 ml/4 tbsp olive oil
150 g/5 oz cooked ham or bacon
1 clove garlic
parsley
sage
rosemary
1 small chilli pepper
salt
60 g/2½ oz (¾ cup) freshly grated Parmesan,
    pecorino romano or similar cheese

Soak the dried beans and drain, then cook in fresh water for about 1 hour. Heat the oil in another pan and add the ham or bacon cut into matchsticks and the finely chopped garlic and herbs. Cook for 5 minutes, then add the drained beans and the chilli pepper. Taste and add salt if necessary. Cook for 10 minutes, adding a little water if the mixture becomes too dry.
Meanwhile, cook the pasta, taking care not to overcook. Drain and turn into a heated serving bowl. Stir in the freshly grated cheese and then add the bean mixture. Remove the chilli pepper, stir well and serve at once.

Pasta e Fagioli
Pasta and Beans

This is a Neapolitan version of this popular combination.

400 g/14 oz mixed pasta or any short pasta
300 g/10 oz (1½ cups) dried beans
60 ml/4 tbsp olive oil
2 cloves garlic
1 stick celery
230 g/8 oz tin Italian plum tomatoes
5 ml/1 tsp tomato paste
½ small chilli pepper salt

Soak the dried beans and drain, then cook in fresh water for about 1 hour. While the beans are cooking, heat the oil and add the quartered garlic and chopped celery. When the garlic turns colour, remove it. Add the chopped tomatoes with their juice, tomato paste, chilli pepper, 100 ml/3½ fl oz water and salt to taste. Simmer for 10 minutes.
About 15 minutes before the beans are cooked, add the tomato mixture to the pan and cook together for the last 15 minutes. Remove the chilli.
A small quantity of beans and tomato are usually puréed to help the sauce coat the pasta. Return to the boil and add the pasta. Have boiling water ready to add if necessary but the finished dish should consist of almost 'dry' pasta in a thick sauce. When the pasta is cooked leave covered for 10 minutes, then serve.

Pasta e Fagioli
Pasta and Bean Broth

This version, from Venice, is almost a broth.

300 g/10 oz tagliatelle
300 g/10 oz (1½ cups) dried beans
200 g/7 oz bacon
1 ham bone, if available
90 ml/6 tbsp olive oil
1 onion carrot stick celery
salt and black pepper
100 g/4 oz (1¼ cups) freshly grated Parmesan cheese

Soak the dried beans and drain, then put into a large saucepan with the chopped bacon, ham bone, oil and chopped vegetables. Cover with cold water and simmer gently with the lid on for 2½ hours. Add salt to taste.
Remove the bone and purée half the mixture. Return the puréed mixture to the pan, bring back to the boil and add the pasta. When the pasta is cooking, check that you do not need to add boiling water, remembering that the finished dish will not be drained and should be a thick broth. Season with a little freshly ground black pepper and serve. The freshly grated Parmesan cheese is usually served separately.

Tuna
Tonno

*T*he tuna is still fished off the south coast of Italy, and the whole bloody ritual of the great kill, the *tonnara*, with its arabic terms and stylized movements, follows age-old custom. Aeschylus refers to this slaughter when he writes of the Persians at Salamis, and both Aristotle and Pliny included long, often erroneous, accounts of the migration habits of the tunny fish.

Fresh tuna can be bought in Italian markets. Succulent steaks are cut from the huge fish as it lies glistening on the slab, next to the more baleful-looking swordfish. But fresh tuna is very expensive in Italy, and the delectable pasta sauces are made with tinned tuna. Tuna in oil gives a richer flavour, but tuna packed in brine can be substituted quite successfully.

Tagliatelle al Tonno
Tagliatelle with Tuna

A fast uncooked sauce, this takes no more time than the tagliatelle.

> 500 g/1 lb tagliatelle
> 200 g/7 oz tin tuna fish
> 60 g/2½ oz (½ cup) shelled walnuts
> grated rind of 1 lemon
> 5 ml/1 tsp Worcestershire sauce
> 60 ml/4 tbsp chopped parsley
> 4 basil leaves, if available
> 180 ml/6 fl oz olive oil
> salt and black pepper

Put the drained tuna, walnuts, lemon rind, Worcestershire sauce and herbs into the food processor or blender and process until smooth. Add the olive oil gradually, and adjust the seasoning.

Cook the pasta, following the packet directions carefully to avoid overcooking. Drain and stir in the tuna sauce, taking care to coat each strand of the pasta with the sauce. Serve immediately.

Spaghetti al Tonno e Limone
Spaghetti with Tuna and Lemon

500 g/1 lb spaghetti
30 ml/2 tbsp olive oil
1 clove garlic
60 ml/4 tbsp chopped parsley
200 g/7 oz tin tuna fish
juice of 1 lemon
60 g/2½ oz (¾ cup) freshly grated Parmesan cheese
30 g/1 oz (2 tbsp) butter
salt and black pepper

Heat the olive oil and add the finely chopped garlic and parsley. Stir continually over
a low heat, gradually adding the drained and flaked tuna fish. The heat should
remain low so that none of the ingredients changes colour.
Cook the pasta, following the packet directions carefully to avoid overcooking.
Drain the pasta and turn into a heated serving dish. Add the sauce and stir well.
Now add the lemon juice, freshly grated cheese, the butter divided into small pieces
and salt and freshly ground black pepper to taste. Stir well and serve at once.
Another more strongly-flavoured version of this sauce can be made leaving out the
cheese and butter, and adding 3 chopped anchovy fillets and ½ small chilli pepper
to the intial frying of garlic and parsley.

Linguine al Tonno e Pomodoro
Linguine with Tuna and Tomato

500 g/1 lb linguine or spaghetti
30 ml/2 tbsp olive oil
1 medium onion
2 cloves garlic
2 400 g/14 oz tins Italian plum tomatoes
salt and black pepper
200 g/7 oz can tuna fish
30 ml/2 tbsp chopped capers (optional)
60 ml/4 tbsp chopped parsley

Heat the oil and gently fry the chopped onion and garlic until softened. Add the
tomatoes with their juice and salt and pepper to taste and cook on a high flame for
10 minutes, stirring occasionally. Purée in a food mill, blender or food processor and
return to the pan. Add the drained and flaked tuna fish and capers and cook for a
further 10 minutes.
Cook the pasta following the packet directions carefully to avoid overcooking.
Drain and add the sauce. Stir well and add the chopped parsley. Cheese is not served
with this recipe.

Shellfish
Frutti di Mare

*F*iumicino to most people means Rome's international airport, but to Romans it means the small fishing port where the fishermen sell their catch all along the quay and the local trattorie turn it into delicious food. 'Il Pescatore' serves pasta with the most exquisite shellfish sauces. Alberto and Domenico Zafrani have generously given me the recipes for three of my longtime favourites, and many of their recipes appear on the menus of 'Sandro's' in Manhattan and 'La Genova' in London.

Spaghetti al Cartoccio
Spaghetti with Shellfish in Foil

This recipe, from 'Il Pescatore', can be made with any mixture of shellfish, so you can adapt the quantities if you do not find all the ingredients. The silver parcel looks spectacular when carried to the table and opened in front of your guests.

> 500 g/1 lb spaghetti
> 500 g/1 lb mussels
> 500 g/1 lb small clams
> 100 g/2 oz tiny squid
> 400 g/14 oz tinned Italian tomatoes
> 1 glass white wine
> 50 ml/3½ tbsp olive oil
> 2 cloves garlic
> 1 small chilli pepper, or 5 ml/1 tsp dried chilli
>   pepper flakes
> 150 g/5 oz unshelled raw prawns or shrimps
> salt
> parsley

Scrub the mussels and clams well with a stiff brush or pot scourer. Discard any mussel or clam that is open or has a broken shell. Put them in a little water over a low heat and cook just until their shells open. This will make sure that any sand comes out and does not go into your pasta sauce. (The shellfish are served in their shells so put small plates on the table for the shells to be discarded as the shellfish are eaten.)

Very small squid are usually served whole. If using larger squid, cut the sack into rings, remove and discard the head and the hard part in the middle of the ring joining the tentacles, and cut the rest into small pieces.

Heat the oil in a large pan and add the chopped garlic and the chilli pepper. When the garlic begins to turn colour add the small squid and the prawns. After 5 minutes add the mussels and clams, tomatoes and wine. Season with salt and cook for 10 minutes.

The spaghetti should be cooked for only half the time stated in the packet instructions. Drain the pasta and very quickly mix it with the hot shellfish sauce and chopped parsley. Have a double layer of foil ready on a baking sheet. Put the spaghetti mixture in the middle and fold over the foil, making sure all the folds are tightly closed to prevent any steam escaping. Cook in a hot oven, 220°C/425°F/ Mark 7, for 8 minutes.

Carry the foil parcel to the table. Open, stir well with a wooden fork and serve from the foil. The aroma that comes out in the cloud of steam has to be experienced to be believed.

Spaghetti alla Crema di Scampi
Spaghetti with Cream and Scampi Sauce

500 g/1 lb spaghetti
40 ml/2½ tbsp olive oil
12 medium sized unshelled raw scampi
1 glass white wine
300 ml/½ pint double cream (1¼ cups heavy cream)
salt and black pepper
parsley

Although the Italian name for these prawns is familiar outside Italy, you may find them sold as Dublin Bay prawns or just giant or king prawns.
Heat the oil in a pan and add the washed scampi heads. Peel the scampi tails, chop them finely and add to the pan. Stir with a wooden spoon for a few minutes then add the white wine. When the wine has evaporated add the cream and bring it to the boil. Simmer for 5 minutes. Season with salt and freshly ground black pepper.
Cook the pasta following packet directions carefully to avoid over-cooking. Drain the pasta, turn into a heated serving dish and stir in the sauce, mixing well until every strand is coated with the sauce. Sprinkle freshly chopped parsley on top and serve at once.

Tagliolini con Gamberi e Radicchio
Tagliolini with Prawns and Radicchio

The strips of pink-coloured radicchio and the coral-coloured prawns make an attractive contrast to the creamy pasta and green of the lettuce.

> 500 g/1 lb tagliolini (tagliarini)
> 60 g/2½ oz (5 tbsp) butter
> 600 g/1¼ lb shelled cooked prawns or shrimps
> 300 g/10 oz radicchio
> 300 g/10 oz lettuce
> 1 small glass brandy
> 150 ml/¼ pint double cream (⅔ cup heavy cream)
> salt and black pepper

Heat the butter and add the prawns and the radicchio and lettuce leaves cut into fine strips. Cook gently for 5 minutes. Add the brandy and when it has evaporated add the cream, salt and freshly ground black pepper.
Cook the tagliolini, following packet directions carefully to avoid overcooking. Drain and stir into the pan containing the prawns. Stir well, place in a heated dish and serve at one.

Pennette alla Ines
Ines's Quills with Shrimp Sauce

Ines Zerbini, who is a natural cook, lives in Ostia Antica and during the summer months is much in demand among the local trattorie where she cooks her fish specialities. The following recipe is simplicity itself.

> 500 g/1 lb pennette or other short pasta
> 500 g/1 lb shelled cooked prawns or shrimps
> 30 ml/2 tbsp olive oil
> 25 g/1 oz (2 tbsp) butter
> 1 small onion
> 1 clove garlic
> 175 ml/6 fl oz tomato sauce (see basic recipe on page 36)
> 1 small glass brandy
> 200 ml/⅓ pint double cream (1 cup heavy cream)
> parsley
> salt and black pepper

Purée half the prawns and chop the rest into medium-sized pieces. Heat the oil and butter and add the finely chopped onion and garlic. When these are soft, add the puréed prawns and tomato sauce. Stir well, then add the chopped prawns and the brandy. When the brandy has evaporated add the cream and chopped parsley. Season with salt and freshly ground black pepper. Keep warm.
Cook the pasta, following packet directions carefully to avoid overcooking. Drain the pasta, turn into a heated serving dish and stir in the sauce. Serve at once.

Penne alla Alberoni
Pasta with Prawns and Mushrooms Baked in the Oven

A recipe from the eighteenth century made for Cardinal Alberoni

500 g/1 lb penne or other short pasta
150 g/5 oz mushrooms
200 g/7 oz (1¾ sticks) butter
salt and black pepper
150 g/5 oz shelled raw prawns or shrimps
1 glass white wine (optional)
25 g/1 oz (2 tbsp) flour
250 ml/8 fl oz milk
grated nutmeg
200 g/7 oz (2½ cups) freshly grated Parmesan cheese
150 g/5 oz mozzarella cheese

Slice the mushrooms finely and fry gently in 30 g/1 oz (2 tbsp) butter. Add salt and freshly ground black pepper. Cook the shelled prawns in the white wine or water and purée them. Make a bechamel sauce with 30 g/1 oz (2 tbsp) butter, the flour and milk and season with salt, pepper and nutmeg. Stir in the puréed prawns, the mushrooms and half the grated Parmesan cheese.
Cook the pasta for half the time stated in the packet instructions.
Drain and stir into the sauce.
Butter an ovenproof dish and add one third of the pasta. Cover with one third of the remaining grated cheese and shredded mozzarella. Dot with a little butter. Now add another layer of pasta, cover as before with the two cheeses and butter, and repeat the process once more. Grind black pepper over the top and bake in a hot oven, 220°C/425°F/Mark 7, for 20 minutes.

Spaghetti con le Cozze o Vongole
Spaghetti with Mussels or Baby Clams

500 g/1 lb spaghetti
1 kg/2 lb mussels or baby clams
30 ml/2 tbsp olive oil
2 cloves garlic
1 small chilli pepper
parsley
salt

Wash the shellfish under running water, scraping the shells with a sharp knife or scourer if necessary. Put them in a large pan with a little water over a gentle heat until they open. Keep the water but strain it to remove any particles of grit.
Heat the oil and add the finely chopped garlic. When the garlic begins to change colour, add the shellfish and a little of their water. Cook gently for about 5 minutes, then add a small piece of chilli. Add salt if necessary. Keep warm.
Cook the pasta, following packet directions carefully to avoid overcooking.
Drain, turn into a heated dish and stir in the sauce. Sprinkle with parsley and serve.

Cheese
Formaggio

*T*he old English stand-by, macaroni cheese, shows that someone at some time or other tried to copy one of the most delightful pasta and cheese recipes from Italy, but achieved only the palest result.

In pasta dishes, the most important cheese is Parmesan. In Italy it is regarded as one of the necessities of life, even mentioned by Boccaccio in the *Decameron*. Parmesan cheese must be bought in the piece and always grated just before use. Now available in most large supermarkets, Parmesan keeps very well wrapped tightly in foil in the refrigerator. Do not be tempted to use ready-grated Parmesan cheese. If you do not have any fresh Parmesan to hand it is better to use a freshly grated substitute cheese or switch menus.

Pecorino romano is a more pungent cheese reserved for the more robust sauces. Parmesan can be used in place of pecorino romano if the latter proves difficult to find, but never substitute pecorino romano for Parmesan. The taste is too strong for many of the more delicate sauces.

Tagliatelle alla Panna
Tagliatelle with Cream and Cheese Sauce

One of the fastest and most delicious of all sauces.

500 g/1 lb tagliatelle
50 g/2 oz (4 tbsp) butter
250 ml/8 fl oz double (heavy) cream
200 g/7 oz (2½ cups) freshly grated Parmesan cheese
black pepper

Melt the butter in a pan and add the cream and half the cheese. Keep warm. Cook the pasta, following packet directions carefully to avoid over-cooking. Drain the pasta and stir in the rest of the butter and cheese. When every strand is coated, stir in the cream sauce. Add freshly ground black pepper to taste and serve at once.

Spaghetti alla Gorgonzola
Spaghetti with Gorgonzola and Ricotta

500 g/1 lb spaghetti
90 g/3½ oz (7 tbsp) butter
1 stalk celery
1 small onion
300 ml/½ pint (1¼ cups) milk
150 g/5 oz gorgonzola cheese
300 g/10 oz ricotta cheese
salt and black pepper

Heat the butter and add the chopped celery and onion. Cook gently without letting them turn colour. In a blender or food processor, purée together the milk, gorgonzola, ricotta and cooked vegetables. Turn into a saucepan and leave to heat through gently, stirring occasionally. Test for salt.
Cook the pasta, following packet directions carefully to avoid over-cooking. Drain and stir in the butter and the warm cheese mixture. Turn into a heated serving dish, stir well and add black pepper to taste. Serve at once.

Rigatoni ai Quattro Formaggi
Rigatoni with Four Cheeses

500 g/1 lb rigatoni or other short pasta
50 g/2 oz Parmesan cheese
50 g/2 oz Gruyère cheese
50 g/2 oz Edam cheese
50 g/2 oz Fontina cheese
100 g/4 oz (1 stick) butter
black pepper

Grate all the cheeses together. Cook the pasta, following packet directions carefully to avoid over-cooking. In a pan large enough to take all the pasta, heat 25 g/1 oz (2 tbsp) of the butter. Drain the pasta, keeping a small quantity of pasta water for the sauce. Turn the pasta into the large pan containing the melted butter and gradually stir in the rest of the butter and the cheeses. Once the cheese begins to melt remove the pan from the heat. It is important to keep stirring during this process. If the sauce seems too dry add a little of the reserved pasta water. Turn into a heated serving bowl and add freshly ground black pepper to taste. Serve at once.

Ham
Proscuitto

*I*n Italy the types of ham are legion. The most delicately flavoured cured ham – *proscuitto crudo* – comes from Parma or San Daniele near Venice. Sliced wafer-thin by machine, the moist, succulent ham, served with fresh figs or melon makes a delicious summer appetiser. This ham is known as *dolce* – sweet – because it is not as salty as the proscuitto served with pickled artichokes and olives, or the *proscuitto di montagna* which has a much stronger flavour and is usually sliced by hand.

Cooked ham, known as *proscuitto cotto*, is not part of the Italian culinary tradition. However, over the last ten years or so imported cooked ham has become more widely used, not as an alternative to *proscuitto crudo* but as an extra ingredient on a platter of hors d'oeuvre, or *antipasto*.

The first recipe comes from a restaurant outside Rome, along the old Appian Way. Just outside the Aurelian wall amid the catacombs and reminders of early Christian Rome is the crenellated tower of the tomb of the Roman matron, Cecilia Metella. She was the daughter-in-law of the wealthy Crassus, who first financed the young Julius Caesar. Presumably she owes her ostentatiously large memorial to her rich in-laws.

Nearby is a *trattoria* which has a beautiful rose garden with tables around a fountain. Their speciality is served in individual bowls, shaped like the top of the Cecilia Metella tower. It is called *scrigno* which means jewel box, suggesting all the delights concealed under the 'lid' of melted cheese.

Scrigno
Jewel Box Pasta

500 g/1 lb fine green pasta or paglia e fieno
tomato sauce (full quantity of recipe page 36)
200 ml/7 fl oz double (heavy) cream
150 g/5 oz (scant 2 cups) freshly grated Parmesan cheese
6 thin slices ham
300 g/10 oz mozzarella cheese

Set aside 6 tablespoons of the tomato sauce. Stir the cream into the rest of the tomato sauce together with one large spoonful of the grated Parmesan cheese. Simmer for 10 minutes.
Cook the pasta for half the time given in the packet instructions. Drain and add to the tomato and cream sauce, stirring thoroughly.
Butter individual ovenproof bowls and fill two-thirds full with the pasta mixture. Cover each serving with a slice of ham cut into six pieces to make it easier to eat when cooked. Now cover this with thin slices of mozzarella. Put the reserved tomato sauce on top and then sprinkle with the remaining Parmesan cheese. Cook in a hot oven, 220°C/425°F/Mark 7, for 20 mintues.

Paglia e Fieno alla Ciociara
Paglia e Fieno Farmhouse Style

A *ciociara* is the long wooden shoe originally worn by farm-workers outside Rome.
The name has been given to a quick, easy sauce that is a favourite.

500 g/1 lb paglia e fieno or tagliatelle
150 g/5 oz (1 cup) shelled peas (fresh or frozen)
25 g/1 oz (2 tbsp) butter
150 g/5 oz white mushrooms
200 g/7 oz ham
250 ml/8 fl oz double (heavy) cream
100 g/4 oz (1¼ cups) freshly grated Parmesan cheese
salt and black pepper

If using fresh peas, cook in a little boiling water for 10 minutes; drain. Melt the
butter and add the peas and sliced mushrooms. After 5 minutes, add the chopped
ham and stir for a few minutes before adding the cream. Add salt and keep warm.
Cook the pasta following packet directions carefully to avoid over-cooking. Drain
and turn into a heated serving dish. Add the grated cheese and stir rapidly. Pour on
the sauce, mix well, add freshly ground black pepper to taste and serve at once.

Soufflé di Tagliatelle
Soufflé of Tagliatelle

This pasta dish has an interesting texture and appearance. The mixture should come to
1 cm/½ inch below the top of the dish before going into the oven.

500 g/1 lb tagliatelle or paglia e fieno
80 g/3 oz (6 tbsp) butter
60 g/2 oz (5 tbsp) flour
300 ml/½ pint (1¼ cups) milk
60 g/2½ oz (⅔ cup) freshly grated cheese, preferably
    Parmesan
3 egg yolks
200 g/7 oz ham
salt black pepper nutmeg
grated nutmeg
6 egg whites

Melt the butter in a small pan and gradually add the flour, stirring continually.
Gradually stir in the tepid milk and stir until you have a smooth sauce. Remove
from the heat.
Cook the pasta for half the time given in the packet instructions; drain.
Stir the cheese and beaten egg yolks into the white sauce and then the ham, cut into
fine strips. Season to taste with salt, pepper and nutmeg. Stir in the drained pasta.
Butter a 1½ pint soufflé dish. Beat the egg whites until they are stiff, then very
gently fold into the pasta mixture. Spoon the mixture into the buttered dish and
cook in a moderate oven, 180°C/350°F/Mark 4, without opening the door,
for 30 minutes. Serve at once.

Tagliatelle alla Papalina
Tagliatelle Papal Style

The Rome trattoria 'La Cisterna' made this sauce for Cardinal Pacelli who used to be a frequent patron. When he became Pope the sauce was dedicated to him and named *Papalina*.

> 500 g/1 lb tagliatelle
> 200 g/7 oz ham
> 1 small onion
> 150 g/5 oz (10 tbsp) butter
> 4 eggs
> 200 ml/7 fl oz cream
> 100 g/4 oz (1¼ cups) freshly grated Parmesan cheese
> salt and black pepper

Cut the ham into fine strips and chop the onion very finely. Melt half the butter and gently cook the onion until it becomes transparent. Add the ham and cook gently for 5 minutes. Keep hot. Beat the eggs together with the cream and half the cheese.
Cook the pasta, following packet directions carefully to avoid over-cooking.
Meanwhile, melt the remaining butter in a large pan and add the egg mixture.
Remove from the heat at once. Add salt to taste.
Drain the pasta and turn into the large pan containing the egg mixture. Stir well.
Now add the hot ham and onion mixture and keep stirring until the hot pasta and ham have caused the eggs to coagulate and form a thick yellow cream.
Turn into a heated serving bowl, add black pepper to taste and serve at once.
The remaining grated cheese should be served separately.

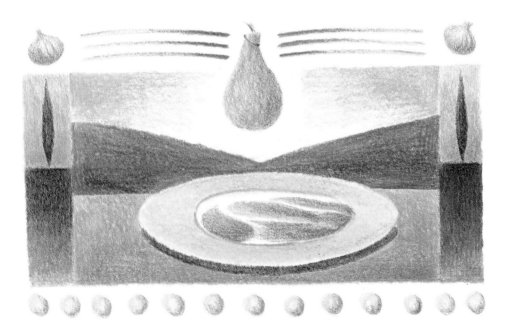

Sausages
Salsiccie

Norcia in Umbria is the home of such excellent pork products that in central Italy a shop specialising in sausages and hams is called a *norceria* and a pasta sauce made from fresh sausages is called *norcina*. Italian sausages are made solely from meat and since they contain quite a lot of fat they are pricked before being cooked slowly in white wine, to enable the fat to run out. For these recipes use good quality meat sausages without additional bread or soya filler.

Rigatoni alla Norcina
Rigatoni with Norcia Sauce

500 g/1 lb rigatoni or short pasta
1 small onion
15 ml/1 tbsp olive oil
200 g/7 oz pork sausages
100 ml/4 fl oz white wine
250 ml/8 fl oz double (heavy) cream
50 g/2 oz (generous ½ cup) freshly grated Parmesan cheese
salt and black pepper

Slice the onion very finely and fry slowly in the olive oil in a covered pan. The onion should not be allowed to change colour. Remove the skin from the sausages and divide the meat into very small pieces. Put them in the pan with the onion and add the wine. After 10 minutes, add the cream and simmer gently, uncovered, for about 10 minutes. Remove from heat, add salt to taste, and keep warm.
Cook the pasta, following packet directions carefully to avoid over-cooking. Drain the pasta, toss in the grated cheese and turn into a heated serving dish. Stir in the sauce, add freshly ground black pepper to taste and serve at once.

Conchiglie alla Burina
Shells with Rustic Sauce

The countryman who sold his butter, or *burro* in Roman markets was called a *burino*, but in modern Rome the term merely means bad-mannered. This sauce takes its name from the original meaning.

500 g/1 lb conchiglie or other short pasta
40 g/1½ oz (3 tbsp) butter
1 small onion
1 clove garlic
400 g/14 oz tinned Italian plum tomatoes
salt and black pepper
200 g/7 oz large pork sausages
1 glass white wine
150 g/5 oz (1 cup) shelled peas

Melt the butter and add the finely chopped onion and garlic. When the onion begins to turn colour add the tomatoes with their juice. Season to taste with salt and black pepper. Cook for 20 minutes.
Meanwhile, prick the sausages and cook them gently in the wine in a separate covered pan. When they are cooked, strain their liquid into the tomatoes. Skin the sausages and slice them into rounds.
Cook the pasta, following the packet directions carefully to avoid over-cooking. Add the peas to the tomato sauce and cook until just tender. Before draining the pasta add the sausage to the sauce. Drain the pasta, turn into a warm serving dish and stir in the sauce. Serve at once.

Bacon
Pancetta

Spaghetti alla Carbonara, or Charcoal-Maker's Spaghetti, is made very quickly from eggs, bacon and cheese. Some experts claim that the sauce was invented by the charcoal workers to sustain them during the long working days on the wooded slopes of the Appenines. Others suggest that the black pepper ground liberally over the finished dish looks like charcoal dust and hence the name. Whatever the real explanation, the sauce is deservedly famous and visitors to Rome can sample it in nearly every *trattoria* including the colourful 'La Carbonara' in Campo dei Fiori, the gastronomic heart of Rome.

The two following recipes are typically Roman and can be found all over the capital. Purists insist that *guanciale*, the tender succulent cut obtained from the pig's cheek, must be used for these sauces, but even in Rome bacon is used just as successfully.

Spaghetti alla Carbonara
Charcoal-Makers' Spaghetti

500 g/1 lb spaghetti
5 eggs
100 ml/4 fl oz double (heavy) cream
salt and black pepper
15 ml/1 tbsp olive oil
25 g/1 oz (2 tbsp) butter
200 g/7 oz streaky bacon
100 g/4 oz (1¼ cups) freshly grated Parmesan and
    pecorino romano cheese, preferably half and half

Beat the eggs and cream together with a pinch of salt. Heat the oil and butter in a large pan. Add the diced bacon and cook gently until the fat becomes transparent. Cook the spaghetti, following packet directions carefully to avoid over-cooking. Drain the pasta and add it to the large bacon pan. Stir well. Remove the pan from the heat and stir in the beaten eggs and cream and a small quantity of the cheese. The eggs will coagulate as they come into contact with the hot pasta so it is very important to work quickly. Stir until each strand of pasta is coated with a thick yellow cream. Now stir in the rest of the cheese and freshly ground black pepper to taste. Serve at once.

Bucatini alla Matriciana
Bucatini Amatrice Style

The ancient Romans turned to the Sabine hills when they needed women, and their descendants in the same spirit have taken the following sauce from the Sabine town of Amatrice to make it irrevocably their own.

500 g/1 lb bucatini or spaghetti
30 ml/2 tbsp olive oil
200 g/7 oz streaky bacon
½ small chilli pepper or 1 teaspoon dried chilli
   pepper flakes
50 ml/3½ tbsp tomato sauce (see recipe page 000)
50 g/2 oz (generous ½ cup) freshly grated pecorino
   romano cheese

Heat the oil and gently cook the bacon cut into thin matchsticks. When the fat begins to become transparent add the chilli and tomato sauce.
Cook the pasta, following packet directions carefully to avoid over-cooking. Drain, stir in the grated cheese and sauce and serve at once.

Meat
Carni

*F*or someone not born in Naples it is difficult to appreciate what *ragù* signifies to a Neapolitan. At one time it was the traditional Sunday lunch for a large part of Naples and for many the one time in the week they could allow themselves the luxury of eating meat. The aroma of *ragù* used to drift along the narrow winding alleys and up over the roof tops until it seemed to many the perfume of Sunday. The *ragù* needs long slow cooking and to avoid burning it needs to be watched as carefully as a new-born baby, as the Neapolitans say. Since this watching period lasts for about three or four hours, it demands patience and a high degree of dedication. Gradually cooking *ragù* came to be seen as an expression of love, care and affection.

The great Neapolitan playwright, Eduardo de Filippo, shows this in a delightful little poem. The speaker criticises his wife's *ragù* saying that his mother made real *ragù* while his wife only produces meat and tomatoes. Clearly it is not only her cooking that is being held in question.

In Naples today, with all the pressures of modern life, the making of the real *ragù* is reserved for special occasions. Puppa Sicca learned to cook *ragù* as a present for her future husband before their formal engagement was announced. She usually makes it three or four times a year and I felt a great sense of warmth and affection when she prepared it for me one day. Here is her recipe. Readers familiar with Eduardo de Filippo's play, 'Saturday, Sunday, Monday', can compare notes.

Zitoni col Ragù Napoletano
Zitoni with Neapolitan Meat Sauce

500 g/1 lb zitoni or spaghetti
1 piece of fresh leg of pork, about 700 g/1½ lb
300 g/10 oz rib pork chops all in one piece
60 g/2½ oz (5 tbsp) butter
60 g/2½ oz (5 tbsp) margarine
100 ml/4 fl oz olive oil
1 onion
1 carrot
1 skinned Neapolitan salami (if available)
1 wineglass white wine
1 wineglass red wine
400 g/14 oz (1½ cups) tomato paste
1 bay leaf
salt and black pepper

This is traditionally cooked in an earthenware pot but any large heavy pan may be used. Tie the pork leg very firmly to keep it in shape. Put the butter, margarine, oil, chopped onion and carrot, bay leaf and meat (with the salami if used) into the pan and begin to cook very gently, covered. This initial cooking period takes about 2 hours. From time to time turn the pieces of meat to brown them on all sides. As the meat gradually browns the onion will disappear.

Now is the time to take the lid off and start adding liquid to make the sauce. As the meat begins to stick, add the white wine a few drops at a time, stirring well with a wooden spoon all along the bottom of the pan. Continue in this way until all the white wine has been used. Now start adding the red wine while scraping the juices from the bottom of the pan in exactly the same way. When the red wine has evaporated, gradually add the tomato paste, stirring it in thoroughly.

When the tomato has become very dark a little tepid water is gradually added. This period of gradually adding water usually takes another 3 hours. The sauce is now very dark. At this stage it may be left to cook on its own. Add about 1.5 litres/ 2½ pints (1½ quarts) of water and cook very slowly in the covered pan for another 4 or 5 hours, stirring every half hour or so. This process is known onomatopoeiacally as *pippiare*. As the meat begins to come away from the bones, remove the pork chops from the pan; the larger piece of pork leg can be removed an hour or two later. Check for seasoning, add salt and black.

The first part of this cooking is usually done the day before and the last few hours on the day itself, but there is no reason why it all should not be cooked in advance. Cook the pasta just before the meal in the usual way, following packet directions carefully to avoid over-cooking. Drain, turn into a serving bowl and stir in the meat sauce. The meat is served separately as a second course.

Fusilli con Polpettine
Fusilli with Meat Balls

Several times I have heard experts on Italian cooking state categorically that spaghetti and meat balls is an American innovation unknown in Italy. Not true, however.
It is important to remember that Italy is divided by its geography, history and culture and only became unified, politically speaking, in the last century. Culinary traditions are still very regional.
A Florentine may never have eaten pasta with meat balls but it is common in the south which was the birthplace of many Italian Americans. In Puglia, meat balls are cooked in a tomato sauce and either eaten with the pasta or served separately afterwards.
The traditional Carnevale Lasagne from Naples always contains meat balls, and they are found in several other recipes in southern Italy.

500 g/1 lb fusilli or other short pasta
2 cloves garlic
400 g/14 oz lean boneless veal, beef or pork
2 small slices white bread, crusts removed
parsley
100 g/4 oz (1¼ cups) freshly grated Parmesan cheese
2 eggs
salt and black pepper
flour
50 ml/3½ tbsp olive oil
1 onion
1 wineglass white wine
400 g/14 oz tinned Italian plum tomatoes
stock

Work the garlic and meat in a food processor or through a mincer (grinder), then add the bread, chopped parsley and half the grated cheese. Mix thoroughly with the eggs and season to taste. Roll into small balls about the size of a walnut and flour lightly.
Heat the oil, add the finely chopped onion and cook until it has softened but not turned colour. Add the meat balls and cook over a low heat until lightly browned on all sides. Now add the wine and boil to reduce to half the quantity. Add the sieved or processed tinned tomatoes and a very little stock. Cover and cook for about 1 hour.
Cook the pasta following packet directions carefully to avoid over-cooking.
Drain and turn into a warmed serving bowl. Stir in the sauce and meat balls and the rest of the cheese and serve.

Tagliatelle Verdi alla Bolognese

Green Tagliatelle with Bolognese Sauce

Bolognese must be the most well-known of all Italian pasta sauces and certainly the most falsified. Counterfeit Bolognese sauce appears on menus all over the world and should usually be avoided. I am tempted to say only eat Bolognese sauce if you are in or around Bologna, or if you have made it yourself. Any sauce using minced (ground) meat does not automatically qualify to be called Bolognese, and most of the poor imitations around bear no resemblance to the rich, opulent sauce which is the triumph of the glorious Emilian cooking tradition.

500 g/1 lb green tagliatelle or egg pasta
150 g/5 oz lean boneless pork
150 g/5 oz lean boneless beef
30 ml/2 tbsp olive oil
80 g/3 oz (6 tbsp) butter
1 medium onion
1 carrot 1 stalk celery

100 g/4 oz bacon
50 g/2 oz fresh Italian sausage or pure sausage meat
1 wineglass white wine
15 ml/1 tbsp tomato paste
1 wineglass stock
salt and black pepper
75 ml/5 tbsp double (heavy) cream
freshly grated Parmesan cheese (optional)

Select lean pork and beef and mince (grind) it in a food processor or ask the butcher to mince (grind) it for you. Heat the oil and 50 g/2 oz (4 tbsp) butter and add the minced onion, carrot and celery and finely chopped bacon. Cook gently for about 10 minutes, then add the pork and beef, sausage meat with skin removed and wine. Cook gently for a further 10 minutes, stirring from time to time. Now add the tomato paste diluted in the stock. Stir in and add seasoning to taste. Cook gently for 1½ hours.
Stir in the cream and when it has been absorbed by the sauce remove from the heat and keep warm. Cook the pasta following packet directions carefully to avoid over-cooking. Meanwhile, return the sauce to the heat and stir in the remaining butter.
Drain the pasta, turn into a heated serving dish and add the sauce.
This dish is often served without stirring in the sauce: the sauce sits in the middle of the circle of drained pasta. It is probably best to bring the dish to the table in its glory, but stir well before serving. Serve freshly grated cheese separately if desired.

Malloreddus con il Ragù di Agnello alla Sarda
Sardinian Pasta with Lamb Sauce

The life in the interior of Sardinia bears no resemblance to the convivial *dolce vita* of the Costa Smeralda. The land is austere and largely uninhabited. The shepherds lead a nomadic life for long periods of the year to graze their sheep on the poor pasture. Sardinian cooking is based on the rhythms of this life.

Meat is usually roasted in the open air over a spit and the sweet-smelling juniper and olive wood add a particular flavour to the meat. No eggs are used in the traditional pasta, which is made from flour, water, salt and a pinch of saffron. This pasta is rolled into a small oval form called *malloreddus* which means baby calf. A fresh cheese is made from the ewes' milk and the matured Sardinian pecorino (pecorino sardo) is known and appreciated far and wide.

500 g/1 lb malloreddus or other short pasta
1 leg of lamb (approx. 1 kg/2 lb)
2 cloves garlic
few sprigs of rosemary
salt and black pepper
100 ml/4 fl oz olive oil
1 small onion
400 g/14 oz tinned Italian plum tomatoes
50 g/2 oz (generous ½ cup) freshly grated pecorino
    sardo or romano cheese

With a sharp, pointed knife, make several small incisions all along the leg of lamb and insert slivers of garlic and sprigs of rosemary. Rub the leg with salt, pepper and oil. Heat the rest of the oil in a pan that can be transferred to the oven later. Brown the lamb all over, then add the finely sliced onion and the chopped tomatoes with their juice. Add more salt and pepper if necessary. Cover with foil and cook slowly for 2 hours, (gas mark 3, 325°F, 170° C) adding a little water if the sauce becomes too dry. When the meat is cooked the sauce is used with the pasta and the meat is served as the second course.

Cook the pasta, following packet directions carefully to avoid over-cooking. Drain the pasta, reserving 60 ml/4 tbsp of the pasta water to add to the sauce. Turn the pasta into a heated serving bowl and stir in the sauce. Grated cheese should be served separately.

Vermicelli alla Monteroduni
Vermicelli in Monteroduni Style

The Monteroduni Palace in Naples used to belong to a branch of the Pignatelli family, but towards the end of the last century the young prince lost the palace overnight at a game of cards. His widowed mother and all his relatives lost their home but fortunately not the traditional family recipe. This version was kindly given to me by Anna Maria Giovagnoni Visocchi, herself a Pignatelli, who now lives in the original palace.

500 g/1 lb vermicelli
100 g/4 oz lard
1 large onion
100 g/4 oz ham
500 g/1 lb lean boneless pork leg
100 g/4 oz (6 tbsp) tomato paste
salt and black pepper

This recipe is traditionally cooked in a copper pan. Heat the lard and add the finely chopped onion. After 5 minutes add the ham and pork which have been finely chopped in a food processor. Once all the meat has browned, stir in the tomato paste and cook very, very gently for 2 to 3 hours. Check for seasoning. At the end of this cooking period the sauce will be very thick.
Cook the pasta, following packet directions carefully to avoid over-cooking. Drain and turn into a heated serving dish. Stir in the sauce and serve at once.

Pappardelle con la Lepre
Wide Ribbon Pasta with Hare Sauce

500 g/1 lb pappardelle or tagliatelle
30 ml/2 tbsp olive oil
50 g/2 oz (4 tbsp) butter
50 g/2 oz bacon
1 small onion, 1 stalk celery
600 g/1¼ lb meat cut from a hare
salt and black pepper
5 ml/1 tsp thyme
15 ml/1 tbsp flour
1 wineglass white wine
500 ml/16 fl oz concentrated stock
freshly grated Parmesan cheese to serve

Heat the oil and butter in a pan and gently fry the finely chopped bacon, onion and celery. Add the meat cut into very small cubes and season with salt, pepper and thyme. When the meat is browned sprinkle with the flour; stir and brown the flour. Add the wine and when that has almost evaporated add the boiling stock.
Cover and cook gently for 2 hours.
Cook the pasta, following packet directions carefully to avoid over-cooking. Drain and turn into a heated serving bowl. Stir in the sauce. Grated Parmesan cheese should be served separately.

Spaghetti alla Chitarra col Ragù di Maiale

Spaghetti alla Chitarra with Pork Sauce

The Abruzzi is a region of great contrasts stretching from the Adriatic Sea at Pescara to the ski resorts in the Appennines. The cooking of the Abruzzi has long been prized by the rest of Italy. The local pasta speciality is spaghetti alla chitarra. The fresh pasta is made with eggs and rolled out less thinly than for tagliatelle. A traditional instrument made of wood with steel wires stretching from end to end – hence the name *chitarra* or guitar – is used to cut the pasta into long strands. The sheet of pasta is placed on the wires and the rolling pin is rolled up and down over the sheet until the pasta falls in thick, uniform lengths between the wires. If it is not available fine tagliatelle may be used.

> 500 g/1 lb spaghetti alla chitarra or tagliatelle
> 60 g/2½ oz (5 tbsp) lard
> 1 large onion
> 1 small chilli pepper
> 120 g/4 oz minced (ground) pork
> 200 g/7 oz tinned Italian plum tomatoes
> salt
> 100 g/4 oz (1¼ cups) freshly grated pecorino romano
>   or Parmesan cheese

Melt the lard in a pan and add the finely chopped onion and the chilli pepper. After 5 minutes, add the pork and stir around until it begins to brown. Now add the chopped tomatoes with their juice and salt to taste and cook for about 30 minutes.
Cook the pasta, following packet directions carefully to avoid over-cooking. Drain the pasta, turn into a heated serving bowl and stir in the sauce. The grated cheese should be served separately.

Spaghetti con Sugo della Piazzaiola

Spaghetti with Pizzaiola Sauce

Another recipe from the south in which the sauce is used for pasta and the meat is then served separately with vegetables.

> 500 g/1 lb spaghetti
> 50 ml/3½ tbsp olive oil
> water
> 6 thin slices veal or beef
> parsley, salt
> 2 cloves garlic
> 1 g/½ tspn capers
> 400 g/14 oz tinned Italian plum tomatoes
> freshly grated Parmesan cheese (optional)

Put the olive oil and water in a pan and heat together. (This is done because the meat must stew, not fry.) Add the meat with a little chopped parsley, the chopped garlic, capers and tomatoes with their juice. Add salt to taste. Cook gently for 35 minutes.
Cook the pasta, following packet directions carefully to avoid over-cooking. Drain and stir in the sauce. Parmesan cheese is usually served separately.

Rigatoni alla Genovese
Rigatoni with Genovese Sauce

This is one of the main Neapolitan sauces and plays an important role in the history of the cooking of Naples yet it is something of a culinary mystery. The name means 'in the style of Genoa' but the sauce itself is unknown in Genoa. The use of onions in this quantity seems to suggest a French influence and the finished dish has certain affinities with Boeuf à la Mode. The most likely explanation seems to be that the sauce was introduced to Naples by one of the many Genoese merchants who settled there in the fifteenth century.

Although this dish is quite time-consuming to prepare, like several other recipes from the south of Italy, it supplies both first and second course. The sauce is used with pasta and the meat is then sliced and served with different vegetables afterwards.

500 g/1 lb rigatoni or any other short pasta
1 small carrot
1 stalk celery
100 g/4 oz raw ham with rind
2 kg/4 lb onions
100 ml/4 fl oz olive oil
1 kg/2 lb lean cut of beef such as topside (top round),
    tied with string to keep its shape
1 wineglass water
salt and black pepper
1 wineglass white wine
stock
100 g/4 oz (1¼ cups) freshly grated Parmesan cheese

Chop the carrot, celery and ham very finely. Thinly slice the onions. Heat the oil in a narrow saucepan just big enough to take the meat and vegetables. When the oil is hot add the ham and chopped vegetables and stir well over a low heat for 5 minutes. Now add the meat and onions. The meat should be completely covered by the onions. Add the water and salt and pepper to taste.

Cover and cook over a moderate heat, stirring from time to time, until the onions and meat begin to turn golden brown. Now turn the heat to very low and begin the slow cooking process. This involves the same techniques as with the Neapolitan *ragù* (see page 101), known as *tirata*, as the flavour is 'pulled' out of the meat into the sauce. A little of the wine and then stock needs to be added each time the sauce is stirred if it appears to be sticking to the bottom of the pan. Stir vigorously under the meat with a wooden spoon at very short intervals because the addition of too much liquid ruins the sauce.

A Neapolitan cook will spend about 2 hours minimum over this part of the recipe. When the cooking process is finished the sauce will be almost chestnut-coloured and the long cooking makes use of the blender or process unnecessary. The sauce can be prepared the day before if required. The meat is usually allowed to cool before slicing.

Cook the pasta following packet directions very carefully to avoid overcooking. Drain, reserving a littlle of the pasta water to add to the sauce before stirring it into the pasta. The Parmesan cheese is stirred into the pasta before the sauce is added or it can be served separately at table.

Special Occasion Pasta
Stravaganze

Bucatini alla Flamande
Bucatini in a Mould

In Naples and the south of Italy there is a strong tradition of ornamental dishes made up of various meat fillings cooked in a pasta mould and then turned out to present a spectacular first course.

Bucatini alla Flamande is an ancient recipe now almost forgotten. No one knows the origin of its name but the recipe itself must date back to the time when the *monzù* – as Neapolitans called their French chefs – were creating masterpieces for the great aristocratic houses.

Prince Francesco d'Avalos first told me of the existence of this recipe, and I am grateful to have learned its secrets from him. The prince's family came to Naples from Spain in the fifteenth century with Alfonso of Aragon and today in the beautiful Palazzo d'Avalos in Naples he and his chef, Herman Piacenti, who prepared this dish for me, still keep the great Neapolitan culinary tradition alive for their appreciative friends.

Tinned copper moulds have been specially made for the Palazzo d'Avalos kitchens by local craftsmen, but the dish can be prepared successfully in a heat-resistant ice cream bombe mould or an ordinary 2 pint (1.2 litres) lidded pudding basin.

I tried this recipe substituting mushrooms for black truffles and found the filling a little anaemic, but the same technique of lining a mould with bucatini can be used to advantage with shellfish or any other special filling when black truffles are not available.

250 g/8 oz bucatini (no other pasta will do)
150 g/5 oz cooked ham
50 g/2 oz cooked tongue
150 g/5 oz cooked chicken breast meat
15 g/½ oz black truffles
200 g/7 oz lean boneless meat
1 carrot
1 onion
1 stalk celery
parsley
2 egg whites
salt and black pepper
500 ml/16 fl oz well-flavoured

For the sauce:
200 g/7 oz meat in one piece
15 ml/1 tbsp olive oil
2 carrots
1 onion
2 stalks celery
1 clove garlic
250 ml/8 fl oz stock
salt and black pepper

Cut the ham and tongue into small cubes and flake the chicken breast. Chop the black truffles. Set these ingredients aside. In a food processor, turn the raw meat, carrot, onion, celery, parsley and egg whites into a fine paste. Season to taste. Add about one-third of the bechamel sauce to the paste in the processor. Keep the paste thick.

To make the sauce, brown the piece of meat in the oil and then add the chopped vegetables. Stir until they are well browned, then add a little stock and cook gently for about 1 hour. Remove the meat and purée the vegetables to make a smooth sauce. Add more stock if necessary. Season to taste.

Cook the bucatini for half the time stated in the packet instructions and then drain. Butter the mould. Take a single strand of bucatini and begin to roll it into a coil in your hand. Place it in the bottom of the mould and gradually coil in more strands of bucatini, sticking them against the buttered sides of the mould to form a lining of coiled bucatini. This is a very slow and fiddly process but the finished effect is worth the effort. Do not worry about the joins in the bucatini; they even out in cooking.

When all the mould has been lined, use a palette knife to plaster the meat and bechamel paste over the bucatini lining, as a brick-layer uses cement. When all the bucatini lining has been pasted firmly to the sides of the mould, begin to fill the mould with a little of the tongue, chicken, ham and truffles, then a spoonful of bechamel sauce and a few strands of bucatini.

Continue this filling process in layers until the mould is full. Finish with a coiled lid of bucatini covered with a generous layer of paste. Cover with buttered paper and then the lid, tied firmly in place.

Cook in a bain-marie of warm water on top of the stove for 45 minutes. At the end of this time, remove the lid and paper and turn out on to a warmed serving plate.

The pasta mould will look like an exotic beehive. I prefer to serve the re-heated sauce separately to avoid masking the beautiful appearance of the unmoulded pasta.

1) Place a coil of pasta in the base of the mould and continue coiling around the sides.

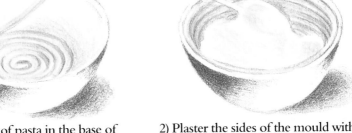

2) Plaster the sides of the mould with the meat paste.

3) Fill the mould with the meat, truffle, and sauce.

4) Finish the 'lid' with a coil of pasta and a layer of meat paste.

Smoked Salmon
Salmone Affumicato

Tagliolini al Salmone
Tagliolini with Smoked Salmon

A luxury sauce prepared in five minutes flat.

500 g/1 lb tagliolini (tagliarini), green if available
30 g/1 oz (2 tbsp) butter
½ small onion
150 g/5 oz smoked salmon
200 ml/7 fl oz single cream
black pepper

Melt the butter and cook the finely chopped onion until it is soft but has not changed colour. Add half the smoked salmon, roughly chopped, and the cream. Warm gently, then blend or process together with the onion until smooth. Cut the rest of the salmon into thin strips, using kitchen scissors.
Cook the pasta, following packet directions carefully to avoid over-cooking. Drain the pasta and turn into a serving bowl. Add the cream and salmon sauce. Stir thoroughly and add a little freshly ground black pepper. Gently stir in the salmon strips and serve at once.

Caviare
Caviale

Spaghetti al Caviale
Spaghetti with Caviare Sauce

500 g/1 lb spaghetti
60 g/2½ oz (5 tbsp) butter
200 ml/7 fl oz double (heavy) cream
black pepper
60 g/2½ oz (¼ cup) caviare
50 g/2 oz smoked salmon (optional extra)

Melt the butter over a low heat, stir in the cream and add freshly ground black pepper to taste. Simmer for 2 minutes and put aside.
Cook the pasta, following packet directions carefully to avoid over-cooking. Meanwhile, return the cream to the heat and stir in the caviare and smoked salmon, cut into thin strips.
Drain the pasta, stir in the sauce, turn on to a heated serving dish and serve at once.

Truffles
Tartufi

A few shavings of fresh truffle turn a simple dish into an opulent, exotic feast. The truffle is particularly suited to dishes of egg, cheese or pasta which act as a neutral foil to set off the heady flavour. White truffles should never be cooked, and black truffles are at their best when merely warmed gently.

The so-called white truffle looks like a clod of earth before it has been cleaned. It should be put in warm water to remove the mud, and any obstinate specks can be removed with a soft brush. Inside it is a delicate camel colour with traceries of fine white veins. Once the outside crust is off, however, it is difficult to notice the appearance. The alluring scent that comes from a truffle in season is an invitation to all the other senses.

White truffles are found mainly around Alba in Piedmont but some are discovered in Umbria near Norcia and Spoleto, the home of the black truffle. The white truffle is in season from October to December, followed by the black truffle in season from Christmas Eve until the end of March. Out of season, truffles have little perfume and are not worth eating, and unfortunately preserved truffles give little idea of the splendour of the fresh truffle.

In the mediaeval city of Spoleto, Emilio Di Marco's restaurant 'Il Tartufo' specialises in truffle dishes. He serves pasta covered with fragrant wafers of large, superbly-flavoured truffles which he buys directly from the local specialists.

Green Tagliatelle with Truffle
Tagliatelle col Tartufo

500 g/1 lb tagliatelle, green if available
100 g/4 oz (1 stick) butter
100 g/4 oz (1¼ cups) freshly grated Parmesan cheese
½ wineglass white wine
salt and black pepper
1 small truffle

Heat 80 g/3 oz (6 tbsp) of butter then stir in the cheese. When this has melted add the white wine, and salt and pepper to taste.
Cook the pasta, following packet directions carefully to avoid over-cooking. Drain and turn into a heated serving dish. Stir in the remaining butter then stir in the sauce. Cover the top with thin shavings of truffle. (In Italy there is a special tool for cutting truffles, but a very sharp paring knife can be used successfully.) Serve immediately.

Soufflé
Soufflé

O ne of the many ways to dress up pasta for a party, is to make it the foundation for a soufflé. It was one of the favourite dishes of the late Sir William Walton, the composer, and was prepared for him in his house on the island of Ischia by his cook, Reale.

Zitoni all'Impiedi
Soufflé with Standing-Up Pasta

400 g/14 oz zitoni or wide tube pasta
150 g/5 oz mozzarella cheese
100 g/4 oz cooked ham
50 g/2 oz (4 tbsp) butter
40 g/1½ oz Parmesan cheese

For the soufflé mixture:
75 g/3 oz (6 tbsp) butter
60 g/2½ oz (4½ tbsp) flour
300 ml/½ pint (1¼ cups) milk
6 eggs, separated
75 g/3 oz (1 cup) freshly grated Parmesan cheese
75 g/3 oz (¾ cup) grated emmenthal cheese
parsley
salt and black pepper

Butter a soufflé dish which is 25 cm/10 inches in diameter and 10 cm/4 inches high. Cut the mozzarella and ham into sticks about 8 cm/3¼ inches long. Cook the zitoni whole for a mere 3 minutes. Drain but keep all the water. Cut the pasta into 8 cm/ 3¼ inch lengths so that when stood up in the soufflé dish they come about 2 cm/¾ inch below the top. Now reheat the pasta in its original water (bring to the boil again before adding the pasta), cook for 3 minutes and drain again. Stir in the butter and Parmesan cheese.

Now comes the time-consuming process: stand a line of pasta tubes all around the inside edge of the dish. Inside the pasta make a border of alternating ham and mozzarella sticks. Now make another circle of pasta tubes, and continue like this until there is a space in the middle of about 7 to 8 cm/3 inches in diameter. (Discard any pasta left over.)

Make a bechamel sauce with the butter, flour and milk, and when it has cooled add the beaten egg yolks, the grated cheeses, chopped parsley and salt and pepper to taste. Beat the egg whites until they are stiff, then fold them gently into the cheese mixture. Spoon this mixture into the rings of pasta, making sure that all the tubes of pasta become filled. When all the tubes are full put the remaining soufflé mixture into the empty space in the middle. Put the dish in a slow oven, 150°C/300°F/Mark 2, to bake for about 1 hour; do not open the oven door during this time. Serve immediately.

Crêpes
Crespelle

*C*répes with a fine pasta stuffing make a sumptuous first course for a dinner party. Use tagliolini and choose one of the creamy, delicate sauces. I like to make green crêpes with spinach and basil – spinach for the colour, basil for the flavour – filled with tagliolini in a smoked salmon sauce.

Crespelle Alexander

250 ml/8 fl oz milk
2 eggs
130 g/4½ oz (1 cup) flour
100 g/4 oz spinach, boiled and squeezed dry
8 basil leaves if available
Butter for frying

Blend the ingredients in a food processor or blender. When the batter is smooth, fry in butter in a non-stick pan to make 6 crêpes. The crêpes should be cooked in advance and allowed to cool so that they are easier to handle.
For the pasta filling use Tagliolini al Salmone. The cream-coloured tagliolini make a contrast with the green crêpe and coral-coloured sauce. The secret is to make the smoked salmon sauce in exactly the same quantity as given in the recipe for Tagliolini al Salmone on page 114, but to cook only half the amount of pasta. The extra sauce is used to pour over the crêpes.
Cook the pasta and stir in half the sauce. Put one sixth of the pasta in the middle of a crêpe, roll it up and place it, seam down, in a buttered oven dish long enough to take the six crêpes on one layer. When all six crêpes are stuffed, pour the rest of the sauce over the top and cook in a moderate oven, 180°C/350°F/Mark 4, for 15 minutes. If I am feeling extravagant I buy a small jar of coral salmon eggs and trail them over the top just before serving.

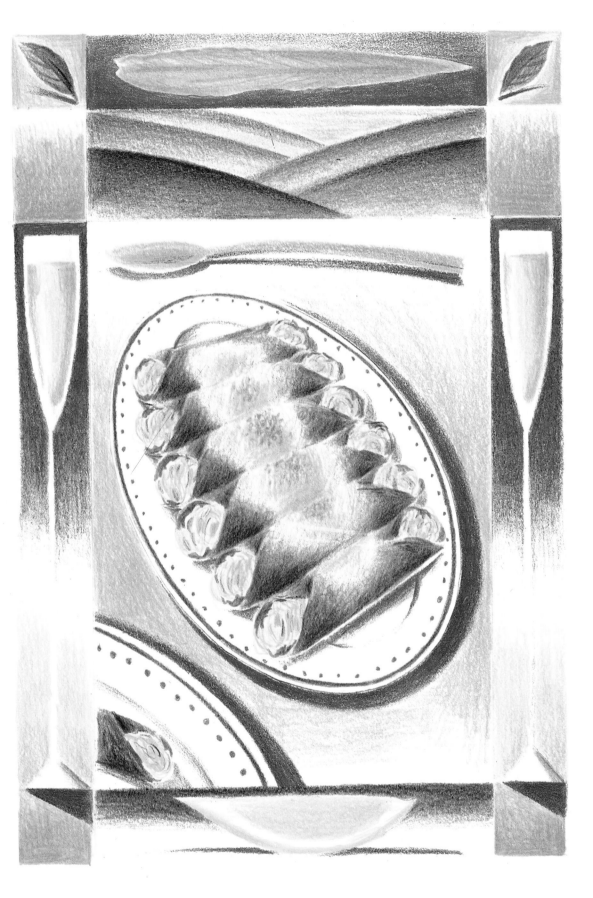

Pastry Cases
Timballi

*F*or important occasions pasta is traditionally served inside a pastry case. Giuseppe di Lampedusa in 'The Leopard' describes how the Prince delighted his guests by serving macaroni pie at the solemn dinner held on the first night of his visit to his country estate, Donnafugata, in Sicily:

Three lackeys in green, gold and powder entered, each holding a great silver dish containing a towering macaroni pie.

The pie crust was always made from sweet pastry in contrast to the savoury filling inside:

Good manners apart, though, the aspect of those monumental dishes of macaroni was worthy of the quivers of admiration they evoked. The burnished gold of the crusts, the fragrance of sugar and cinnamon they exuded, were but preludes to the delights released from the interior when the knife broke the crust; first came a spice-laden haze, then chicken livers, hard boiled eggs, sliced ham, chicken and truffles in masses of piping hot, glistening macaroni, to which the meat juice gave an exquisite hue of suede.

Timballo del Gattopardo

Timballo from 'The Leopard'

For the pastry:
500 g/1 lb (3½ cups) flour
pinch of salt
5 ml/1 tsp ground cinnamon
150 g/5 oz (¾ cup) sugar
150 g/5 oz (10 tbsp) butter
water to mix

Filling:
500 g/1 lb short pasta
1 chicken (3 lb/1.35 kilos)
500 g/1 lb piece of beef (optional)
1 stalk celery
1 onion or 2 carrots
5 eggs
100 g/4 oz (1¼ cups) freshly grated Parmesan cheese
salt black pepper parsley
60 ml/4 tbsp olive oil
100 g/4 oz cooked ham
120 g/4½ oz chicken livers
150 g/5 oz (1 cup) shelled peas
1 small black truffle (an optional extra)

I prefer to avoid the sweet/savoury combination so I omit the sugar and cinnamon. Make the pastry and chill for at least 1 hour.

Boil the chicken with the small piece of beef, the celery, onion and carrot. Drain the chicken and strain the stock.

Take 200 g/7 oz (about 1½ cups) of cooked chicken meat and mince (grind) or process it with one egg, two-thirds of the Parmesan, parsley, and salt and pepper to taste. When you have a soft, paste-like consistency, roll it into balls the size of a cherry. Fry the balls in the olive oil; they should barely change colour. Cut the rest of the chicken meat into strips, and cut the ham into similar strips. Simmer the chicken liver for a few moments in a little water with salt and pepper. When cooked cut into small pieces. Cook the peas. Hard boil the remaining eggs. All the above preparation can be done well in advance.

Roll out two-thirds of the pastry to make a circle large enough to line a deep well-buttered oven dish. Roll out the rest of the pastry to make a lid for the pie. Heat 400 ml/14 fl oz of the strained stock and add the chicken, ham, chicken livers, meat balls and peas. Remove from the heat. Add sliced truffles if available. Cook the pasta for half the time stated in the packet instructions; drain. Add half the pasta to the meat mixture and put the other half into the pastry case, arranging it around the outer edges and leaving a space in the middle. Put the pasta and sauce into the middle space and spoon over the top of the plain pasta. Arrange the hard-boiled eggs, each cut into eight segments, over the top and cover with the rest of the grated cheese.

Cover with the other piece of pastry and seal the edges well with a little milk. Bake in a moderate oven, 180°C/350°F/Mark 4, for about 40 minutes.

Timballo per la Domenica delle Palme
Macaroni Pie for Palm Sunday

This is made with fish and is served on Palm Sunday in Naples. Although this recipe traditionally uses a sweet pastry casing, I am giving a version which I think is more acceptable to modern tastes.

For the pastry:
500 g/1 lb (3½ cups) flour
pinch of salt
250 g/8 oz (2 sticks) butter
2 eggs
water to mix

Filling:
500 g/1 lb spaghetti or vermicelli
500 g/1 lb filleted white fish such as cod
100 g/4 oz (1 cup) black olives
45 ml/3 tbsp drained capers
30 g/1 oz (¼ cup) pine nuts, shelled
    walnuts or blanched almonds
parsley
salt and black pepper
250 ml/8 fl oz olive oil
fresh breadcrumbs
100 g/4 oz (⅔ cup) shelled peas
500 ml/16 fl oz tomato sauce (see basic
    recipe page 36)
100 g/4 oz mushrooms
500 g/1 lb shellfish such as mussels,
    clams, etc.
1 tbsp cornflour (cornstarch)
2 cloves garlic
6 anchovy fillets

Make the pastry and chill for at least 1 hour.
Butter a large round ovenproof dish. Roll out two-thirds of the pastry and use to line the dish. Bake blind for 10 minutes in a moderate oven, 180°C/350°F/Mark 4. At the same time, roll out the rest of the pastry to make a large lid for the pie. Put on a greased baking tray and bake at the same time as the pastry case. Remove the case and lid from the oven and allow to cool.
In a food processor, process the raw white fish, pitted olives, capers, nuts, some parsley, and salt and pepper to taste. Add two tablespoons (30 ml) of oil and two tablespoons breadcrumbs. If the mixture seems too wet, add more breadcrumbs.
Roll this mixture into balls the size of a walnut. Coat the balls lightly in breadcrumbs and fry in a little olive oil until they begin to turn colour. Add the fish balls and to the tomato sauce. Leave to cook gently.
Slice the mushrooms and cook lightly in a little oil, then add them to the tomato sauce.
Cook the shellfish in a little water until they have opened. Remove them from their shells and add to the sauce. Strain the cooking liquid and add to the sauce as well.

Stir the cornflour, dissolved in a little cold water, into the sauce to thicken it.
Heat 50 ml/3½ tbsp heat olive oil in separate pan and add the chopped garlic.
When it turns colour, discard it and add the finely chopped anchovies and some
chopped parsley to the oil.
Cook the pasta for half the time given in the packet instructions. Drain and stir in
the anchovy sauce.
Put a layer of pasta in the pastry case, followed by a layer of tomato sauce. Then add
another layer of pasta and another layer of tomato sauce. Finish with a layer of pasta.
Put the pastry lid on top and cook in a moderate oven, 180°C/350°F/Mark 4,
for 40 minutes.

Pasta in Pastry

It is possible to serve any of the more delicate pasta recipes inside a large vol-
au-vent casing. A vol-au-vent filled with small tortellini in the cream, pea
and ham sauce on page 94 makes an elegant first course.

I also like to make a quiche-style pastry case and fill it with small pasta
shells or quills and the courgette (zucchine) sauce on page 44. For an elegant
topping, I arrange thin overlapping slices of courgettes, which have been
cooked for 5 minutes in boiling salted water, over the top of the pasta, cover
by a light sprinkling of Parmesan cheese and black pepper, and bake for 15
minutes in a moderate oven, 180°C/350°F/Mark 4.

Acknowledgements

For many years I have been eating, cooking and talking about pasta with Italian friends. But I would particularly like to thank the following individuals for their help to me during that period that I was writing this book: in Naples, Francesco d'Avalos, Annamaria Visocchi Giovagnoli, Nello Oliviero and Pupa Sicca; in Ischia, Lady Walton; in Lecce, Sandra Della Notte and Emma Guagnano; and in Rome Rita Soccorsi, Ines Zerbini and Angelina di Mambro. Among those who gave me recipes from pasta dishes served in their restaurants, I would like to thank Guiseppe Palladino from 'Vecchia Roma', Filippo Porcelli from 'Checco er Carettiere', and Mario from 'Taverna Guilia', all in Rome. Also Salvatore Mellino from the trattoria, 'Maria Grazia', in Marina di Cantone, Emilio di Marco of 'Il Tartufo' in Spoleto, and Alberto and Domenico Zafrani from 'Il Pescatore' in Fiumicino. My special thanks to Robert Budwig, whose illustrations have so marvellously caught the spirit of Italy and its pasta dishes and to my editor, Maureen Green, for her skill and unfailing encouragement and support.

Diane Seed, 1988

Diane Seed moved to Rome some years after studying English Literature at London University. For fifteen years she taught English at St. George's School, while bringing up her three daughters. With her daughters grown up, she now continues to live in Rome writing for magazines on Italian subjects and her passion for cooking. For this collection of pasta dishes she has drawn on recipes acquired over the years from the farms, palazzos, markets, restaurants and families of her extensive Anglo–Italian circle.

Robert Budwig is design director of "Triangle", a London design company, for whom he has created stationery, fabrics and a range of ceramics which have sold world-wide. After leaving St. Martin's School of Art, he joined Conran Associates and was involved in designing the kitchen section of the Habitat catalogue, among other projects.

He has also contributed to various magazines, including "Good Housekeeping" and "Taste" as a food illustrator and began drawing Italian food on a visit to Tuscany before producing this his first book.